FRANCIS FRITH'S
TOWN & CITY
MEMORIES

MACCLESFIELD

MATTHEW HYDE is a local architectural historian who has published books on Knutsford and Alderley Edge, and is currently engaged on the rewrite of Nikolaus Pevsner's 'South Lancashire'. In the year 2000 he carried out a Millennium spoken history project in conjunction with Macclesfield Museums Trust, resulting in a book and a CD of collected memories.

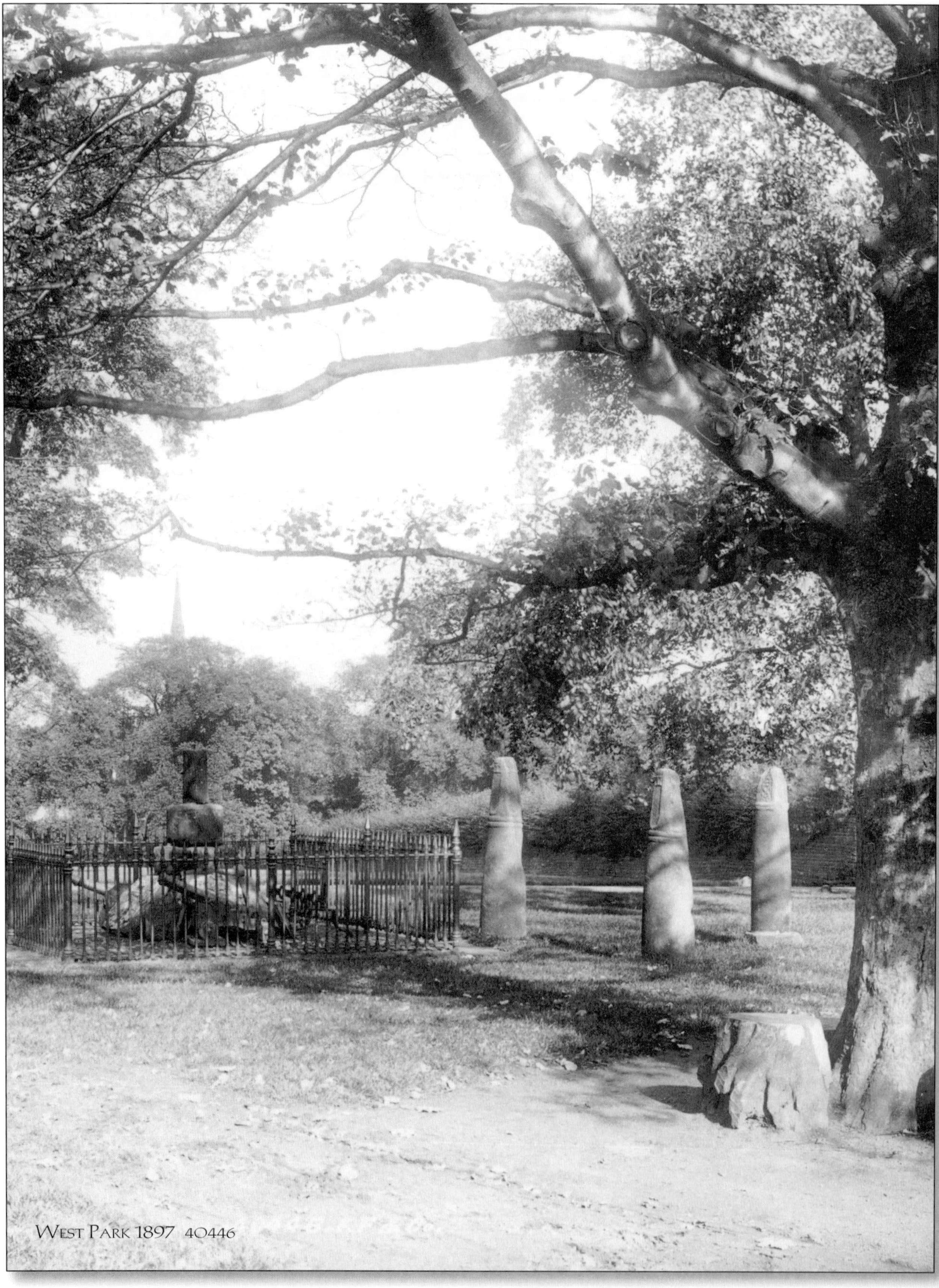

West Park 1897 40446

FRANCIS FRITH'S
TOWN & CITY
MEMORIES

MACCLESFIELD

MATTHEW HYDE

FRANCIS FRITH'S
TOWN & CITY
MEMORIES

First published as Macclesfield, A Photographic History of your Town in 2001 by Black Horse Books, an imprint of The Francis Frith Collection

Revised edition published in the United Kingdom in 2005 by
The Francis Frith Collection as Macclesfield, Town and City Memories.

Limited Hardback Edition 2005
1-84589-013-2

Paperback Edition 2005
ISBN 1-85937-959-1

British Library Cataloguing in Publication Data

Macclesfield
Town and City Memories
Matthew Hyde

The Francis Frith Collection
Frith's Barn, Teffont,
Salisbury, Wiltshire SP3 5QP
Tel: +44 (0) 1722 716 376
Email: info@francisfrith.co.uk
www.francisfrith.co.uk

Aerial photographs reproduced under licence from Simmons Aerofilms Limited
Historical Ordnance Survey maps reproduced under licence from Homecheck.co.uk

Printed and bound in England

Front Cover: Macclesfield, Chestergate 1898 42600t

The colour-tinting in this image is for illustrative purposes only,
and is not intended to be historically accurate

Every attempt has been made to contact copyright holders of illustrative material. We will be happy to give full acknowledgement in future editions for any items not credited. Any information should be directed to The Francis Frith Collection.

AS WITH ANY HISTORICAL DATABASE, THE FRANCIS FRITH ARCHIVE IS CONSTANTLY BEING CORRECTED AND IMPROVED, AND THE PUBLISHERS WOULD WELCOME INFORMATION ON OMISSIONS OR INACCURACIES

FRANCIS FRITH'S

TOWN & CITY

MEMORIES

Contents

The Making of an Archive	6
An Approach from Above	8
Ordnance Survey Map	22
The Market Place	24
Victorian County Map	28
Park Green	34
Macclesfield from the Air	48
Gothic	50
Brabner's Map	58
The West End, Public Works and James Stevens	60
Out in Cheshire	78
Names of Pre-Publication Buyers	84
Index	85
VOUCHER FOR FREE MOUNTED PRINT	89

The Making of an Archive

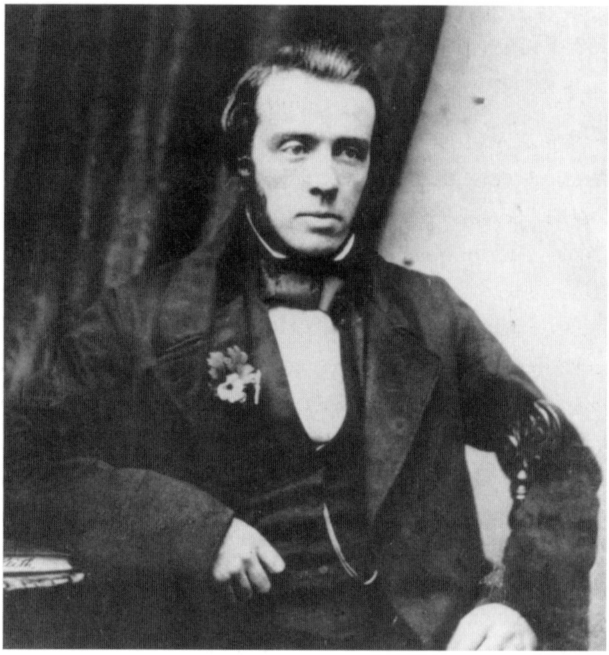

Francis Frith, Victorian founder of the world-famous photographic archive, was a devout Quaker and a highly successful Victorian businessman. By 1860 he was already a multi-millionaire, having established and sold a wholesale grocery business in Liverpool. He had also made a series of pioneering photographic journeys to the Nile region. The images he returned with were the talk of London. An eminent modern historian has likened their impact on the population of the time to that on our own generation of the first photographs taken on the surface of the moon.

Frith had a passion for landscape, and was as equally inspired by the countryside of Britain as he was by the desert regions of the Nile. He resolved to set out on a new career and to use his skills with a camera. He established a business in Reigate as a specialist publisher of topographical photographs.

Frith lived in an era of immense and sometimes violent change. For the poor in the early part of Victoria's reign work was a drudge and the hours long, and ordinary people had precious little free time. Most had not travelled far beyond the boundaries of their own town or village. Mass tourism was in its infancy during the 1860s, but during the next decade the railway network and the establishment of Bank Holidays and half-Saturdays gradually made it possible for the working man and his family to enjoy holidays and to see a little more of the world. With characteristic business acumen, Francis Frith foresaw that these new tourists would enjoy having souvenirs to commemorate their days out. He began selling photo-souvenirs of seaside resorts and beauty spots, which the Victorian public pasted into treasured family albums.

Frith's aim was to photograph every town and village in Britain. For the next thirty years he travelled the country by train and by pony and trap, producing fine photographs of seaside resorts and beauty spots that were keenly bought by millions of Victorians.

The Rise of Frith & Co

Each photograph was taken with tourism in mind, the small team of Frith photographers concentrating on busy shopping streets, beaches, seafronts, picturesque lanes and villages. They also photographed buildings: the Victorian and Edwardian eras were times of huge building activity, and town halls, libraries, post offices, schools and technical colleges were springing up all over the country. They were invariably celebrated by a proud Victorian public, and photo souvenirs – visual records – published by F Frith & Co were sold in their hundreds of thousands. In addition, many new commercial buildings such as hotels, inns and pubs were photographed, often because their owners specifically commissioned Frith postcards or prints of them for re-sale or for publicity purposes.

In order to gain some understanding of the scale of Frith's business one only has to look at the catalogue issued by Frith & Co in 1886: it runs to some 670 pages. By 1890 Frith had created the greatest specialist photographic publishing company in the world, with over 2,000 stockists! The picture on the right shows the Frith & Co display board on the wall of the stockist at Ingleton in the Yorkshire Dales (left of window). Beautifully constructed with a mahogany frame and gilt inserts, it displayed a dozen scenes.

THE MAKING OF AN ARCHIVE

POSTCARD BONANZA

The ever-popular holiday postcard we know today took many years to appear, and F Frith & Co was in the vanguard of its development. Postcards became a hugely popular means of communication and sold in their millions. Frith's company took full advantage of this boom and soon became the major publisher of photographic view postcards.

Francis Frith died in 1898 at his villa in Cannes, his great project still growing. His sons Eustace and Cyril continued their father's monumental task, expanding the number of views offered to the public and recording more and more places in Britain, as the coasts and countryside were opened up to mass travel. The archive Frith created continued in business for another seventy years. By 1970 it contained over a third of a million pictures of 7,000 cities, towns and villages. The massive photographic record Frith has left to us stands as a living monument to a special and very remarkable man.

This book shows your town as it was photographed by this world-famous archive at various periods in its development over the past 150 years. Every photograph was taken for a specific commercial purpose, which explains why the selection may not show every aspect of the town landscape. However, the photographs, compiled from one of the world's most celebrated archives, provide an important and absorbing record of your town.

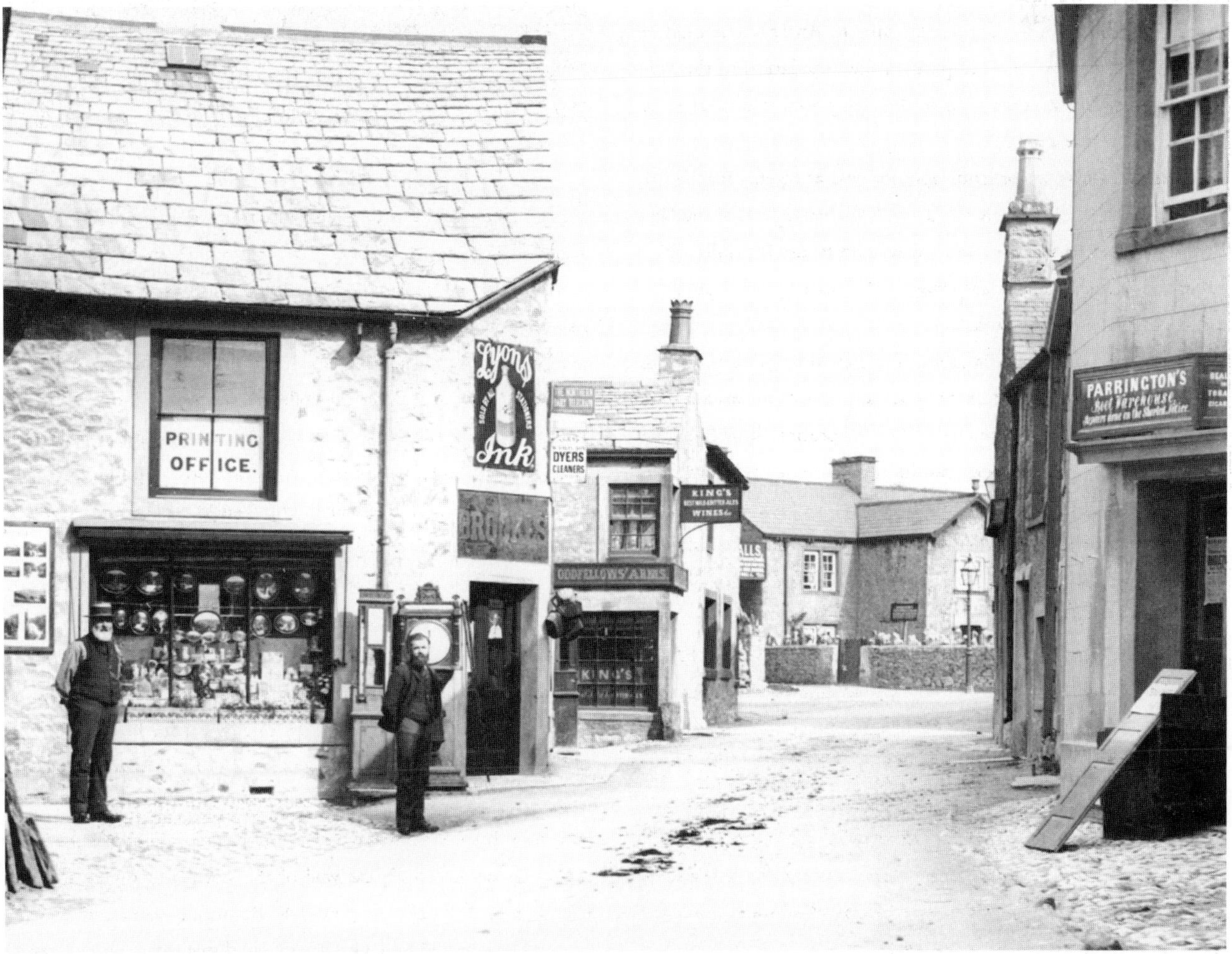

An approach from above

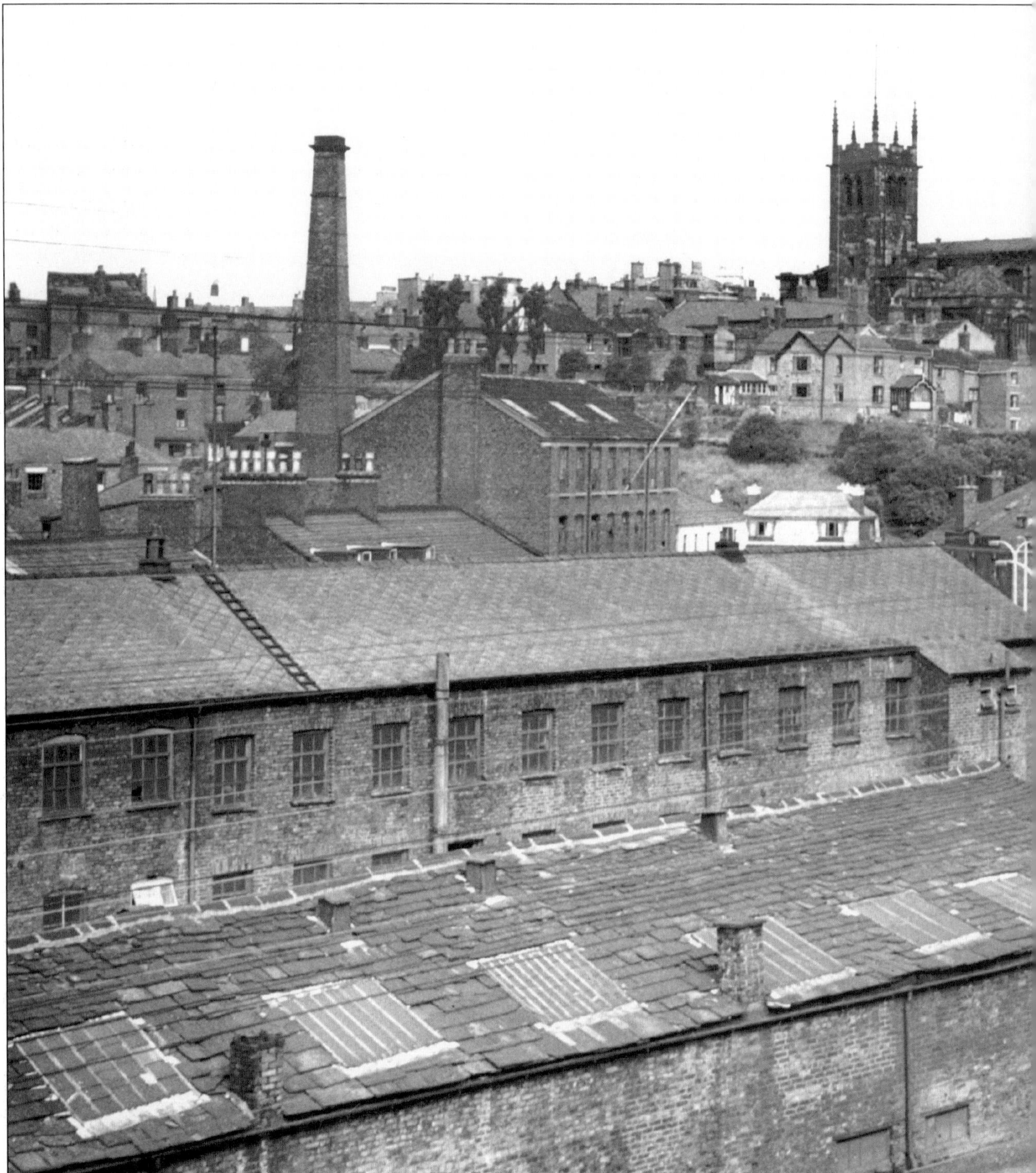

AN APPROACH FROM ABOVE

THE PARISH CHURCH c1955 M2021

This is quintessential Macclesfield, photographed in the dog years between silk town prosperity and south Manchester boom town affluence. The old church stands on its hill, and old houses cluster around. Waters Green is below, ringed with pubs and silk mills. A brief appearance by the river Bollin from under Central Station is indicated by the square of bushes, centre foreground. The scene is now much softened by trees.

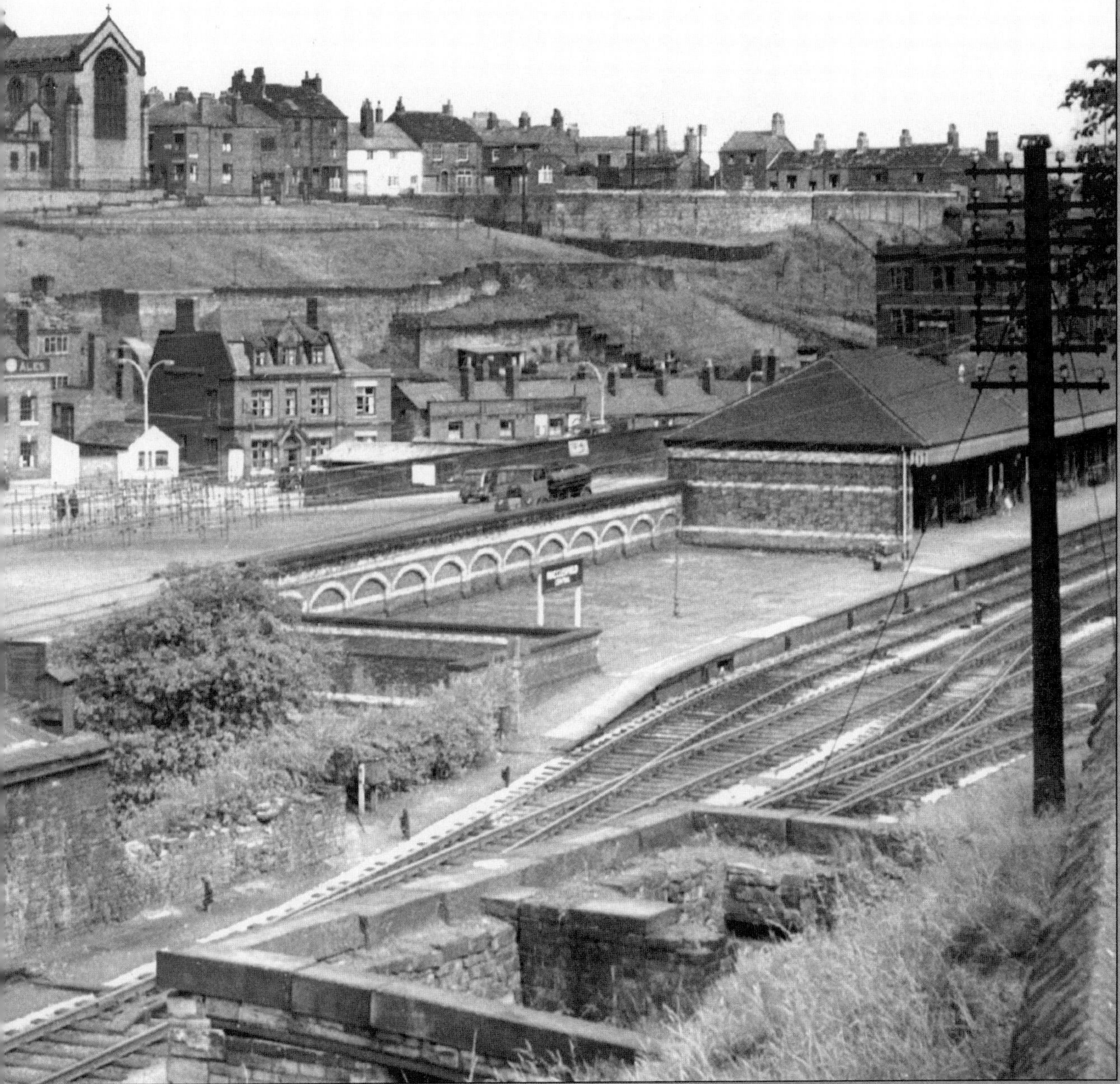

An Approach from Above

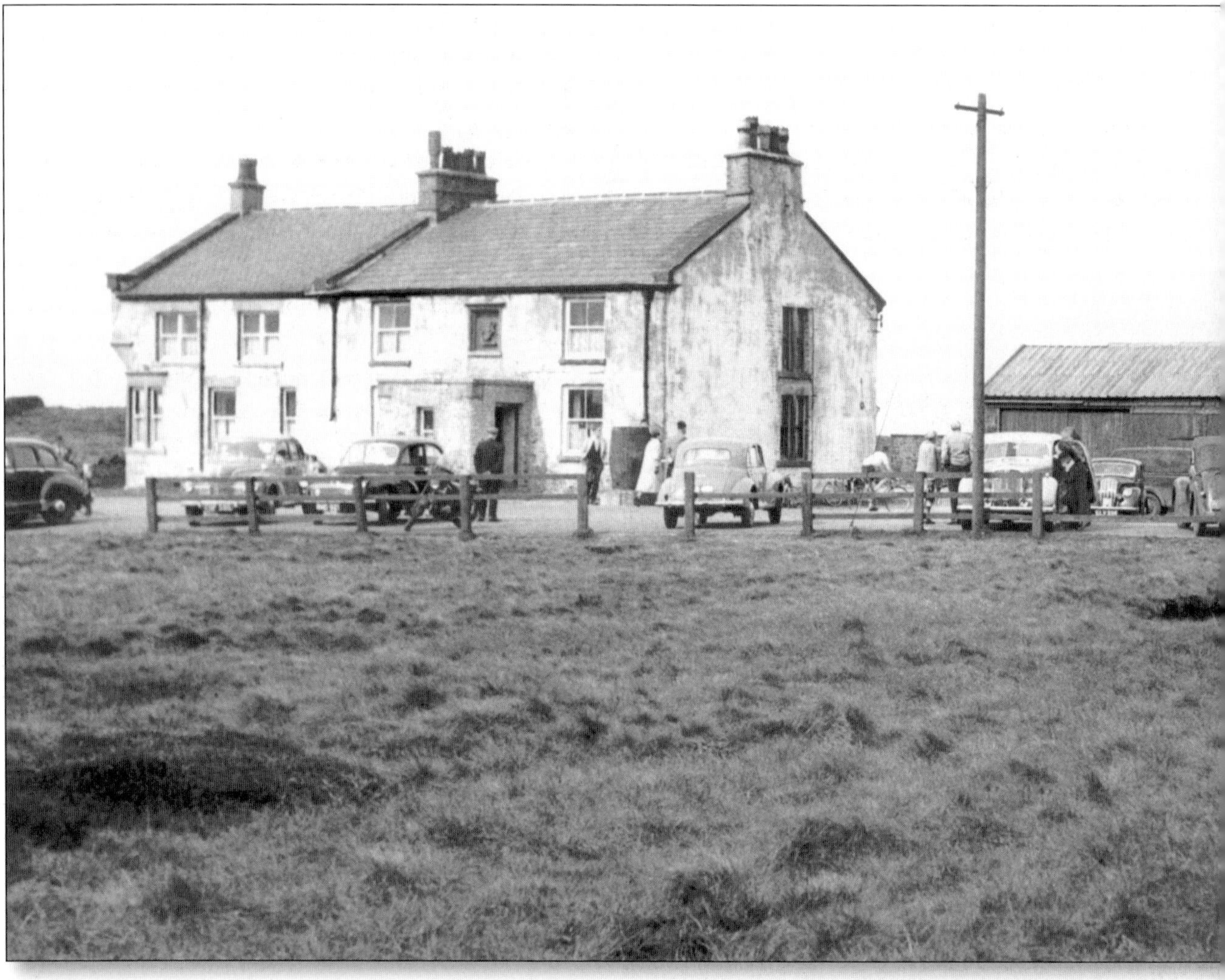

The best way to approach Macclesfield is over the top road from Buxton, as Francis Frith's photographer did in 1955. He evidently paused at the Cat and Fiddle Inn on the summit (M2033, above and M2024 pages 12-13), where on a summer Sunday today rows of gleaming bikes will gather outside. The hills unfold, bleak and bare, and the whole of the Cheshire plain stretches before us far out to the Welsh hills. On a good day we may catch a gleam of silver of the Mersey at Frodsham, and the square tower of Liverpool cathedral can be spied, having been completed against all the odds, during the darkest years of the war.

Suitably refreshed, we begin the long descent. The road was beautifully engineered as long ago as 1830 by Thomas Telford, with lots of sharp bends to even out the gradient (bikers love them!) but in 1897 and 1903 (the dates of the previous visits of Frith photographers), before the age of motor transport, this would still have been a hazardous and difficult route. Even today it is not undertaken lightly in a bad winter.

Soon Manchester comes into view, all black chimneys in 1955, all white towers now. Out in the plain is the feathery crest of the Peckforton Hills and the detached crag of Beeston Castle. Nearer to hand, a startling sight, is the giant dish of Jodrell Bank radio telescope which had been started in 1952 and was nearing

THE CAT AND FIDDLE c1955 M2033

Here we see a good line-up of 1950s transport outside England's highest pub. I wonder which one belonged to the Frith photographer? The pub has been partly rebuilt since 1955, and has lost its shabby whitewash.

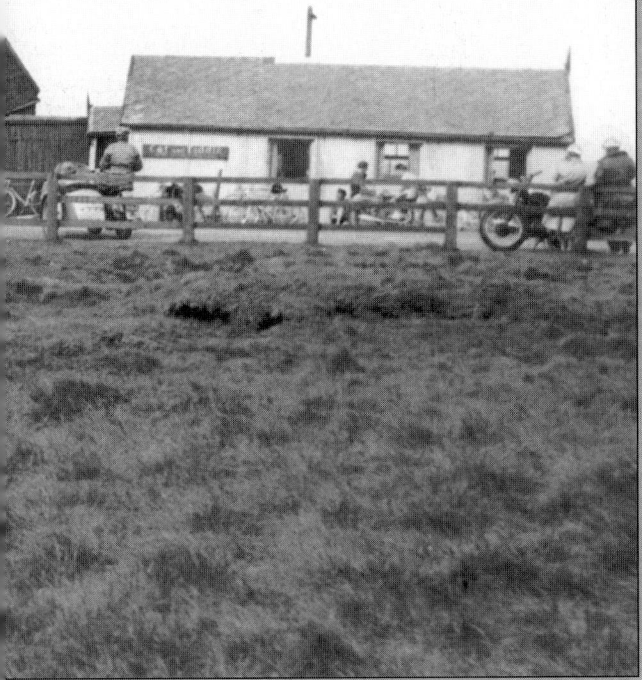

completion in 1955. Sometimes in a low sun the dish itself can look like a crescent moon. Today it is one of Cheshire's great landmarks, and has even been made a listed building. Only as we approach the bottom does Macclesfield appear (M2022, pages 16-17), tucked in against the Pennine slope, densely packed with houses and mills and punctuated by church towers. The Buxton to Macclesfield Road is famously bendy, but the sharpest S-bend of all is near the bottom by the strangely-named One House. It is not really a strange name, for it originally meant exactly that: The One House, the only house, the lonely house. It says a lot about the hazards of the journey in times gone by when there was so little habitation.

We reach the home straight. At the top of it, where the old and the new Buxton Roads converge, is an empty site where once stood the romantically-named Forest Cottage. It was demolished some years ago in the name of road safety, but buses heading this way still bear the legend 'Forest Cottage', proving that words last longer than bricks and mortar. Passing the author's house on the right, we cross the Macclesfield Canal which skirts the town just above the 500-foot contour line. Here stands the Puss in Boots pub. What is the connection between the Buxton Road and nursery rhymes about cats?

Further down is Victoria Park (40458, 49469 and M2031, pages 18-19 and 20-21). The vicar of Birtles recorded in June 1894: 'Whit Monday will always be remembered in Macclesfield. On this day our good parishioner and neighbour, Mr Frank Brocklehurst, formally presented to the town the splendid gift of the new Victoria Park. Bells and bands, bunting, illuminations, fireworks, guns, a general holiday, a procession an hour in length, a most imposing ceremony, the Mayor's banquet, these were only some of the items that rendered the occasion most remarkable. It was a large-hearted and thoughtful gift, and to us locally was not overshadowed by even that other great ceremony which took place the next week - the opening by the Queen of the Manchester Ship Canal'. Immediately below the park was a very dense area of old housing. Many people will remember the names: Waterloo Street, Arbourhay Street, Daybrook Street ... It was all cleared away in the late 1960s in the name of progress, and replaced by the brave new world of the Victoria Park Flats. These were of the infamous deck-access type with flat roofs, and soon began to give trouble. Now the flats in their turn are being demolished, having lasted only thirty years. At the time of writing they are almost gone, and traditional brick houses are being built instead.

Opposite on the Buxton Road are the Brocklehurst or Fence Almshouses (see illustration on page 20), given once again by the family who have had such an influence on the town. The almshouses are built in a very entertaining architectural style which looks particularly good when we get a snowfall. The office block with a running inscription in stone may well be by the Leek architect Sugden. The brick one is by Walter Aston of Bollington, who worked with Richard Harding Watt of Knutsford to such entertaining effect.

An Approach from Above

Ahead of us is the east gable and black tower of St Michael's church, but before we reach it there is one more geographical hazard to be negotiated. The steep valley of the Bollin lies between us and the old town. Today the river is obscured by the railway, and Waters Green has lost its animal sales, but the fair still comes here twice a year as it has done since the town got its charter in 1262. It is a stiffish climb up to the marketplace. Wheeled transport goes round, but the hardy pedestrian climbs straight up the 108 steps to attain, somewhat out of breath, the marketplace.

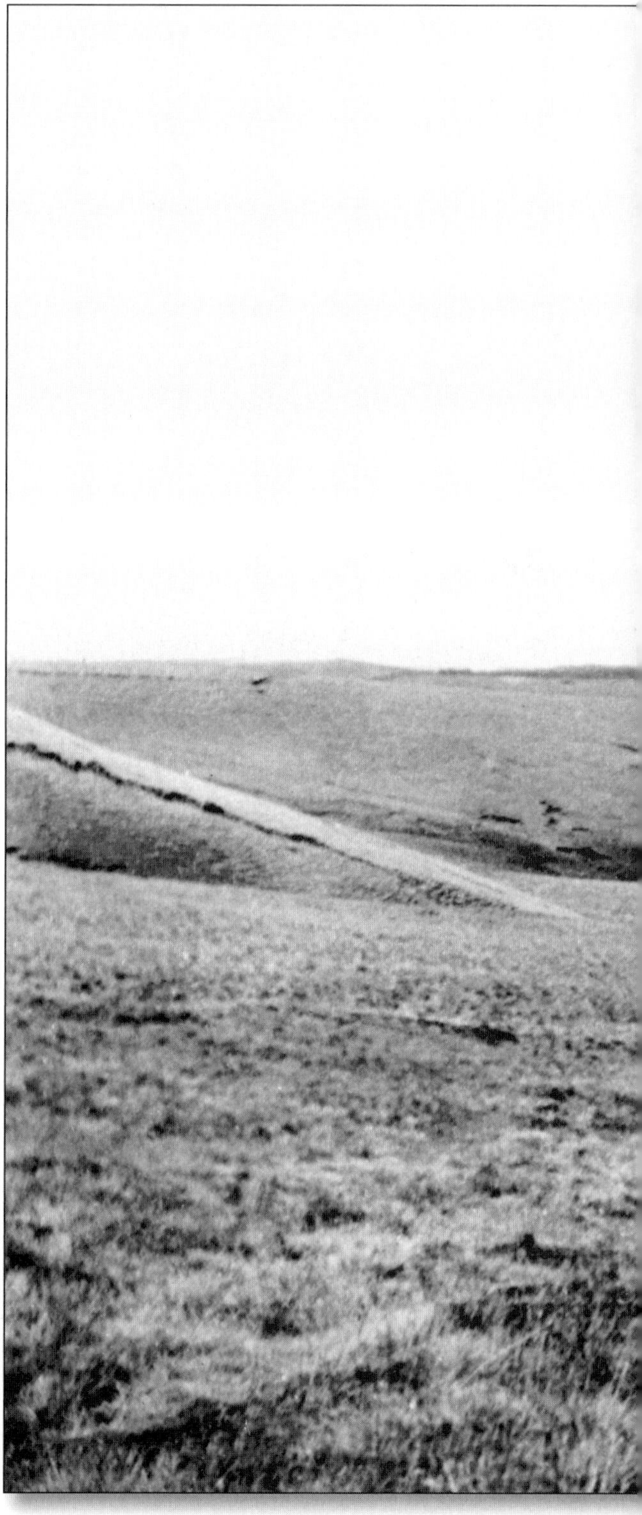

THE VIEW FROM THE CAT AND FIDDLE c1955 M2024

Today the bareness of the landscape is mitigated a little by the conifers of Macclesfield Forest which appear over the far horizon.

MACCLESFIELD

An approach from above

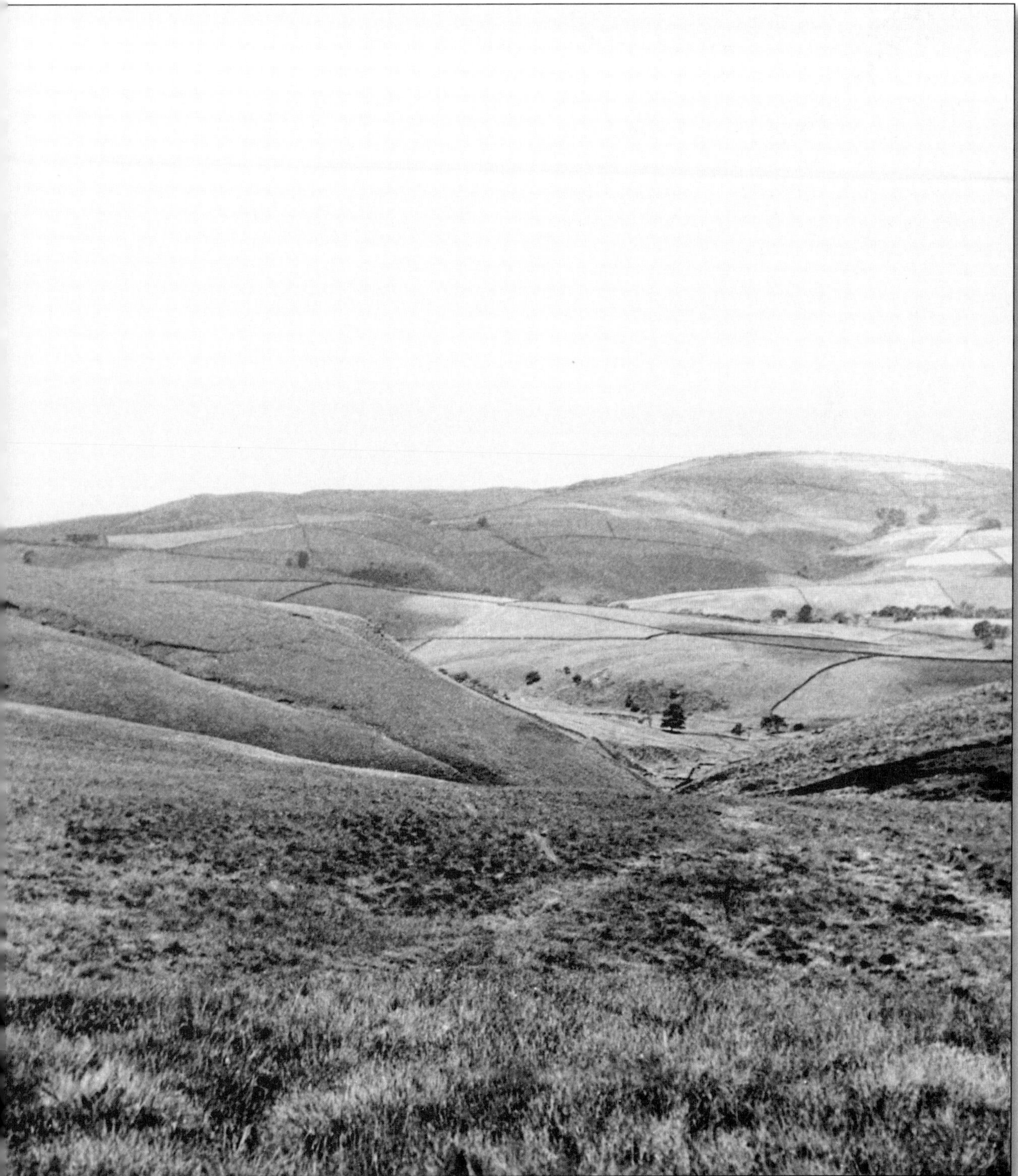

An Approach from Above

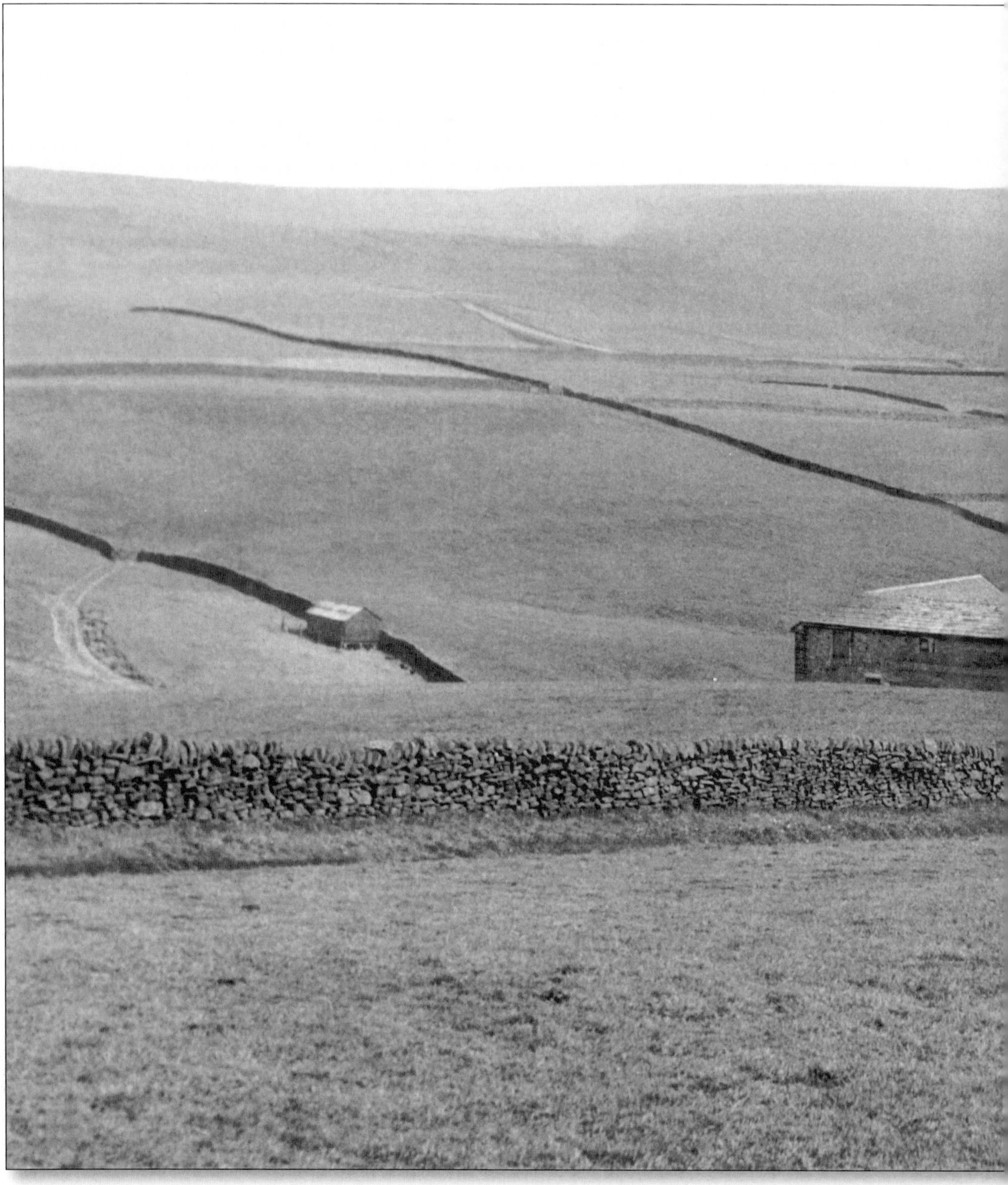

THE VIEW FROM BUXTON ROAD c1955 M2037

Hindsclough Farm is in the foreground, and Shutlingsloe is just out of shot to the right.

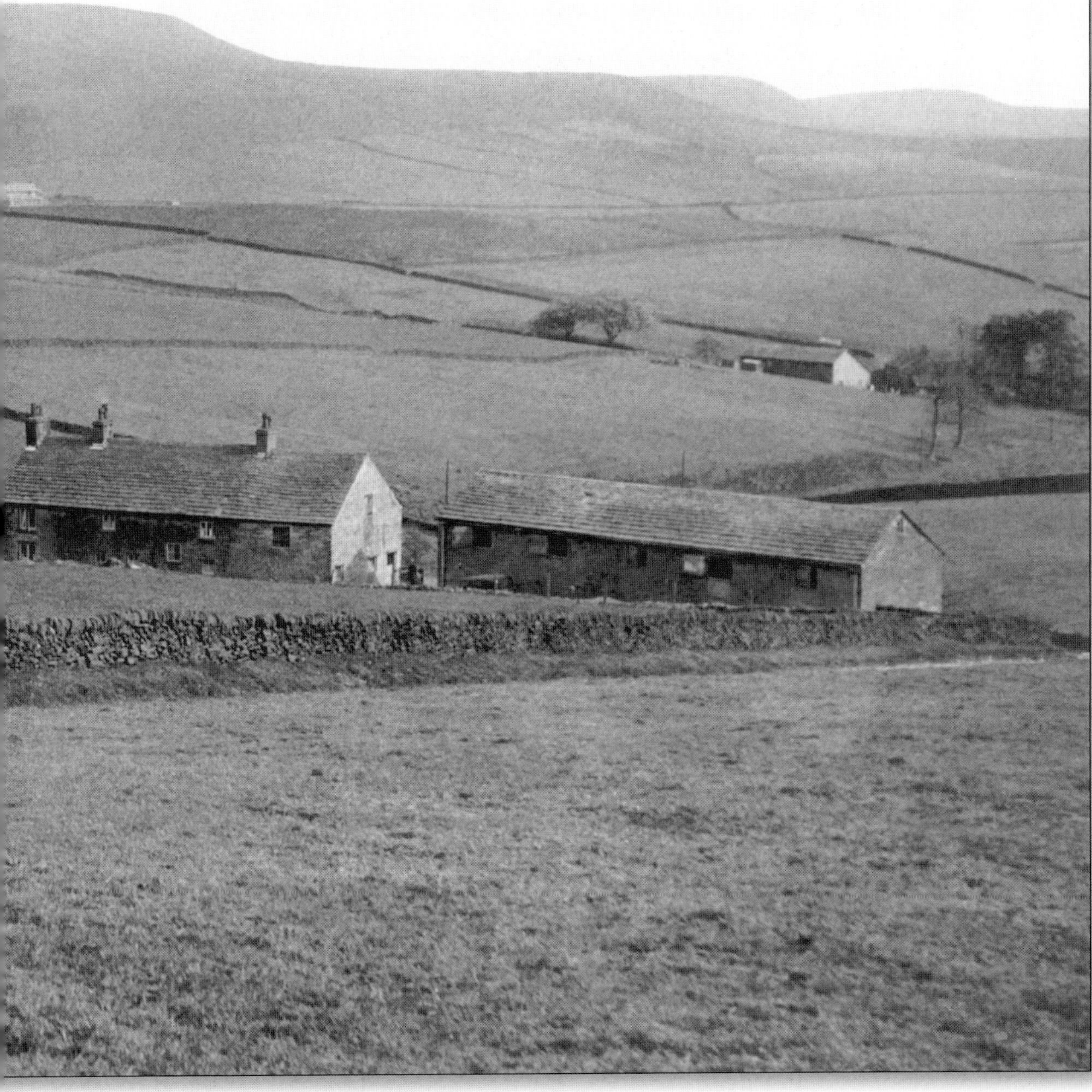

An approach from above

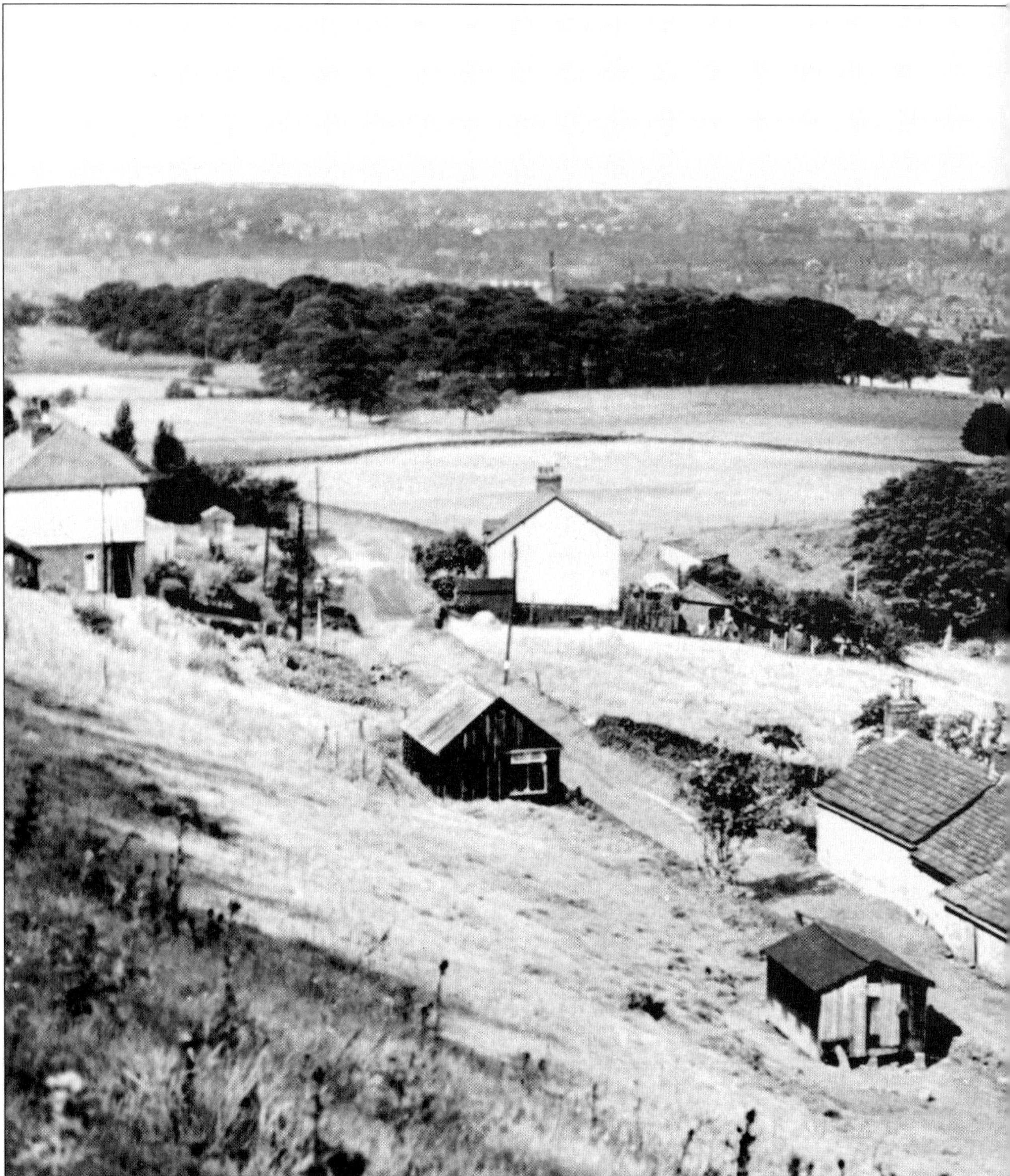

AN APPROACH FROM ABOVE

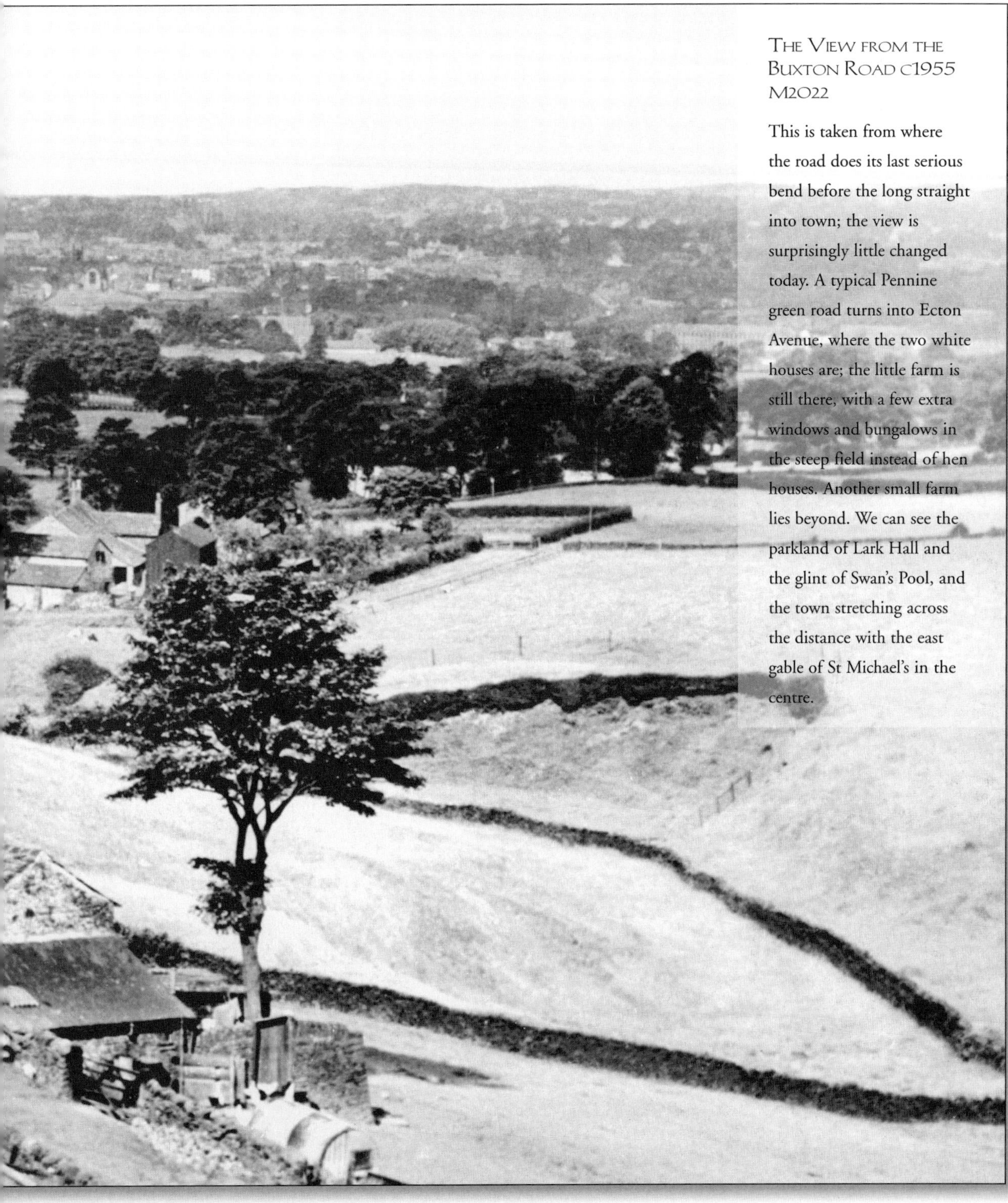

THE VIEW FROM THE BUXTON ROAD c1955 M2022

This is taken from where the road does its last serious bend before the long straight into town; the view is surprisingly little changed today. A typical Pennine green road turns into Ecton Avenue, where the two white houses are; the little farm is still there, with a few extra windows and bungalows in the steep field instead of hen houses. Another small farm lies beyond. We can see the parkland of Lark Hall and the glint of Swan's Pool, and the town stretching across the distance with the east gable of St Michael's in the centre.

AN APPROACH FROM ABOVE

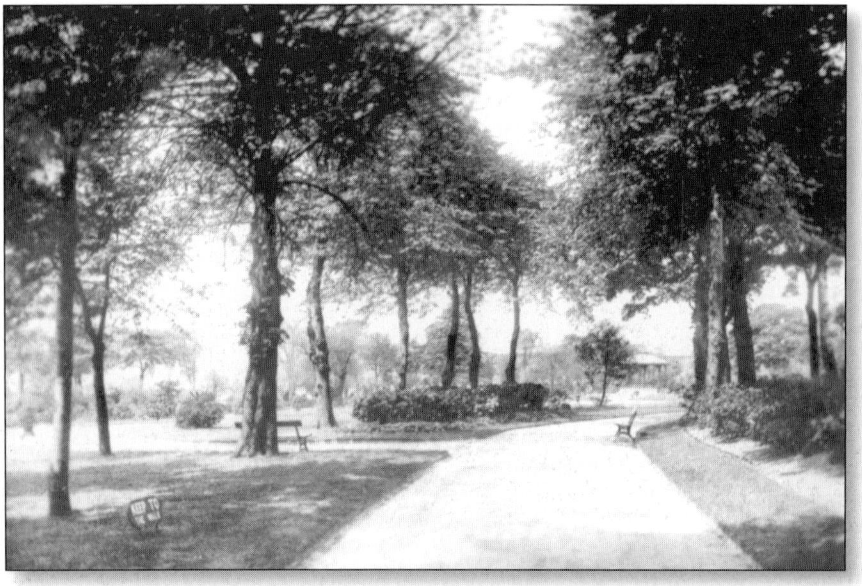

VICTORIA PARK 1903 49469

The bandstand is in the distance. On the far left we can see the stone which records the park's donation to the town, and the spot where the old Brocklehurst house called The Fence stood.

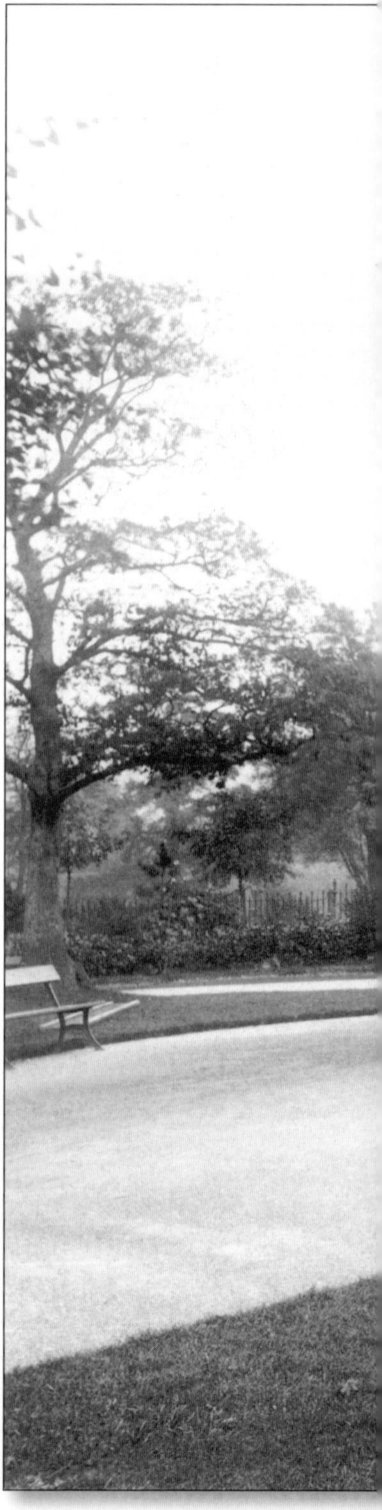

VICTORIA PARK 1897 40458

The park was newly opened at the time of this photograph, and as we can see, it was immaculately kept. Behind the bandstand is the line of Fence Avenue, but there are no houses yet, nor was the High School built. The bandstand has lost a few of its curlicues with the passage of time.

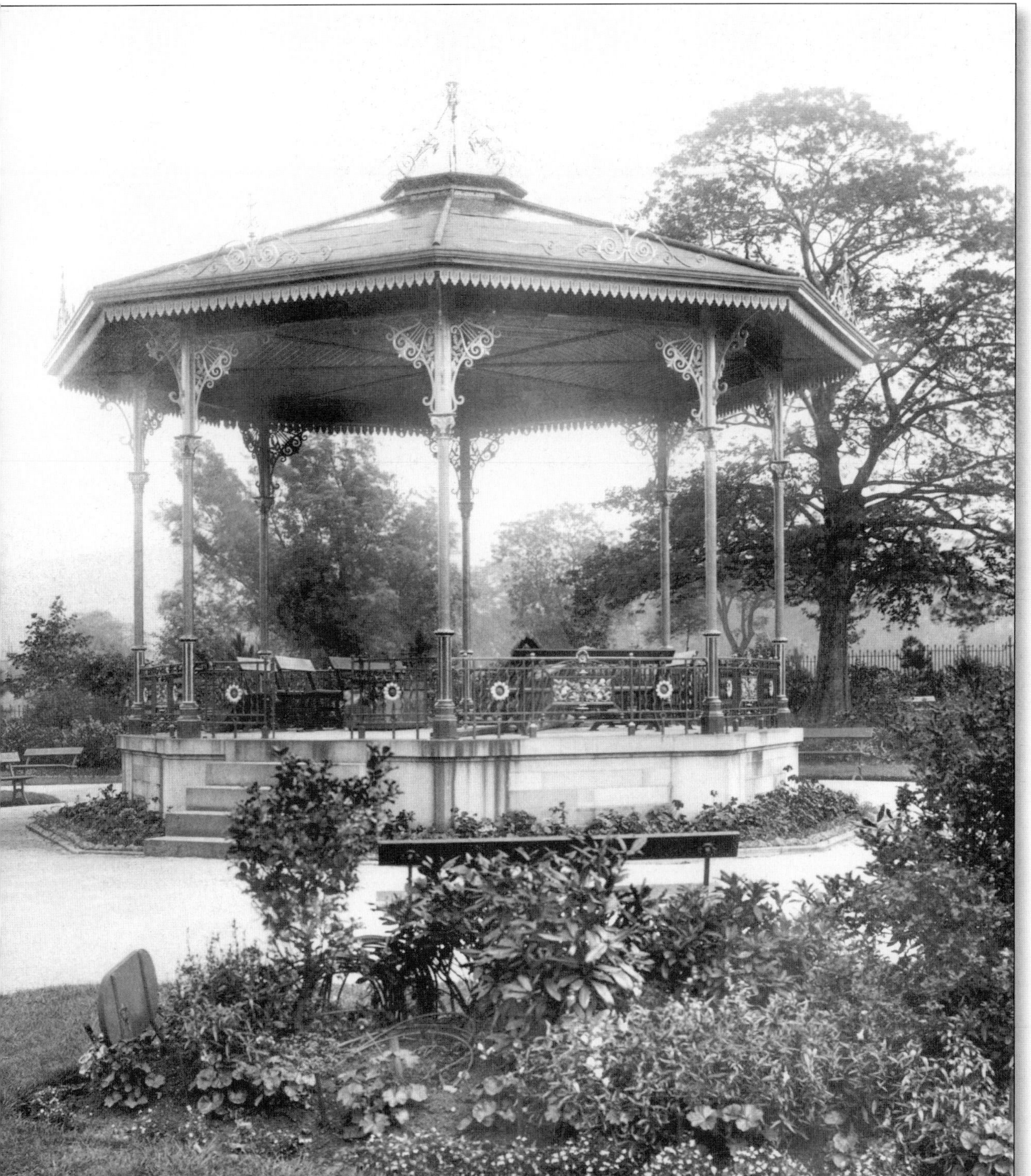

AN APPROACH FROM ABOVE

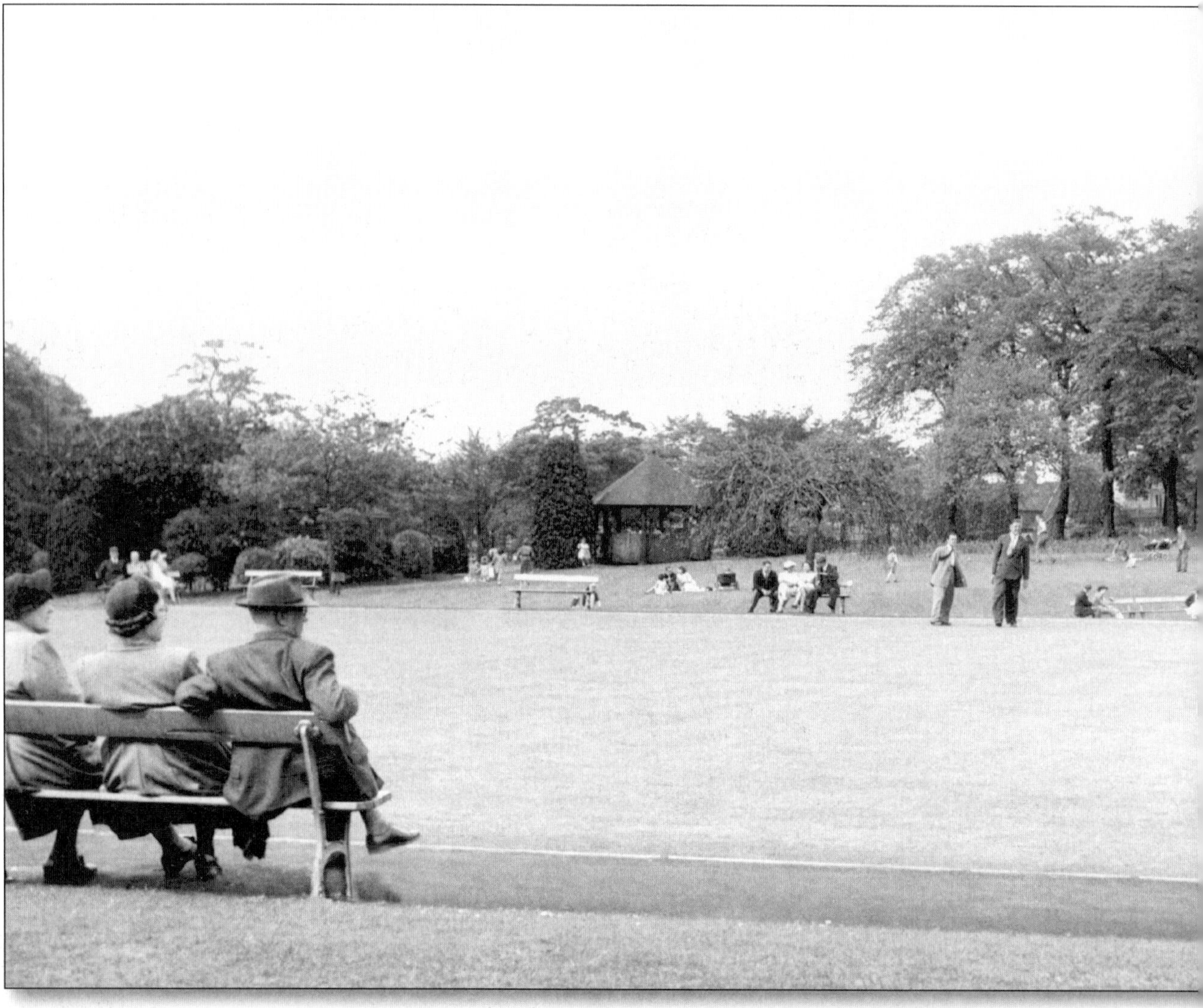

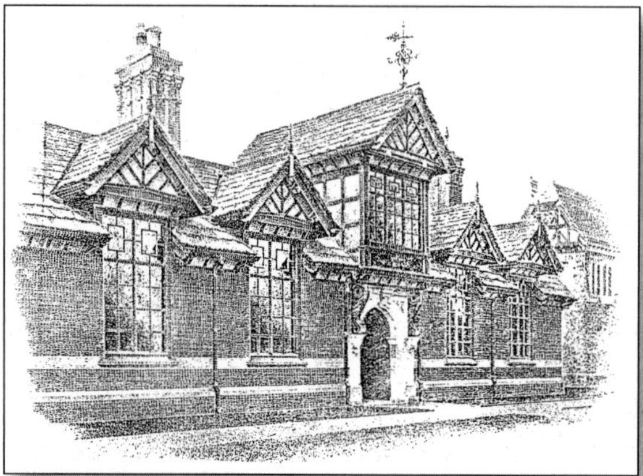

BUXTON ROAD, THE FENCE OR BROCKLEHURST ALMSHOUSES

These almshouses were designed by Walter Aston, a most interesting architect who died tragically young.

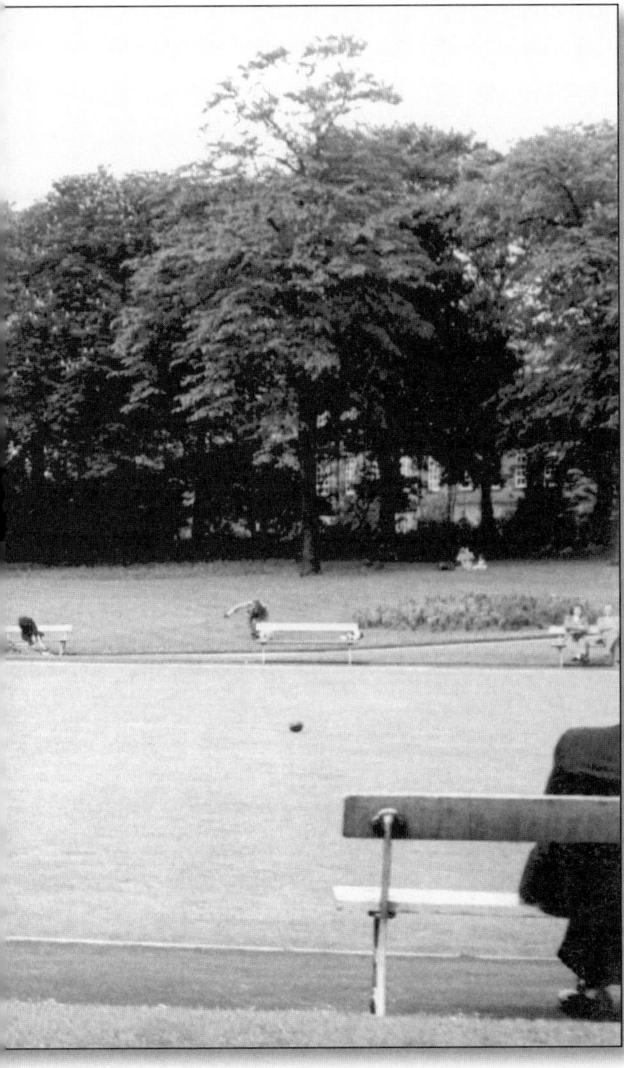

VICTORIA PARK c1955 M2031

From the bowling green we can just see the High School and the houses on Fence Avenue through the trees on the right.

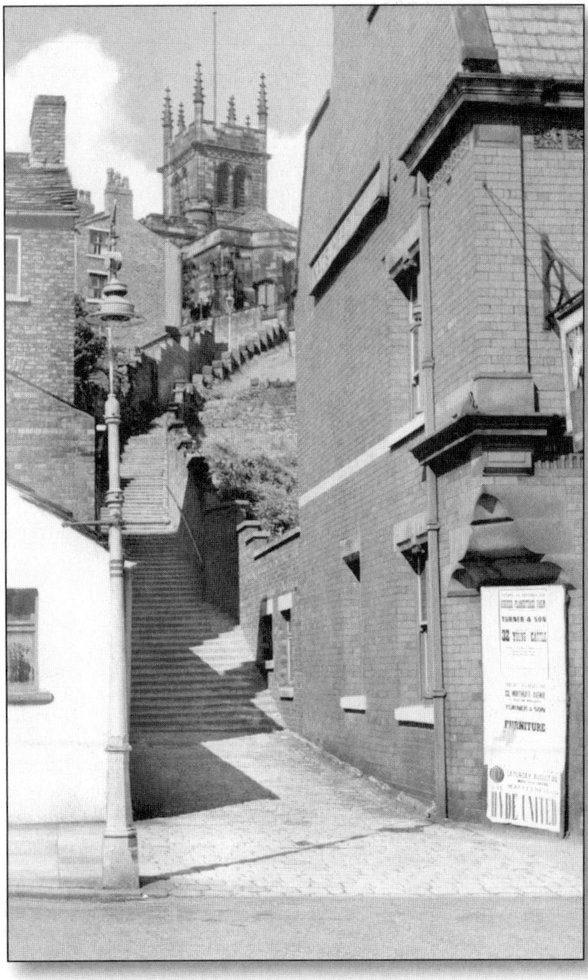

THE 108 STEPS c1955 M2002

Macclesfield's best-known and steepest thoroughfare links Waters Green below with the Market Place above.

Ordnance Survey Map

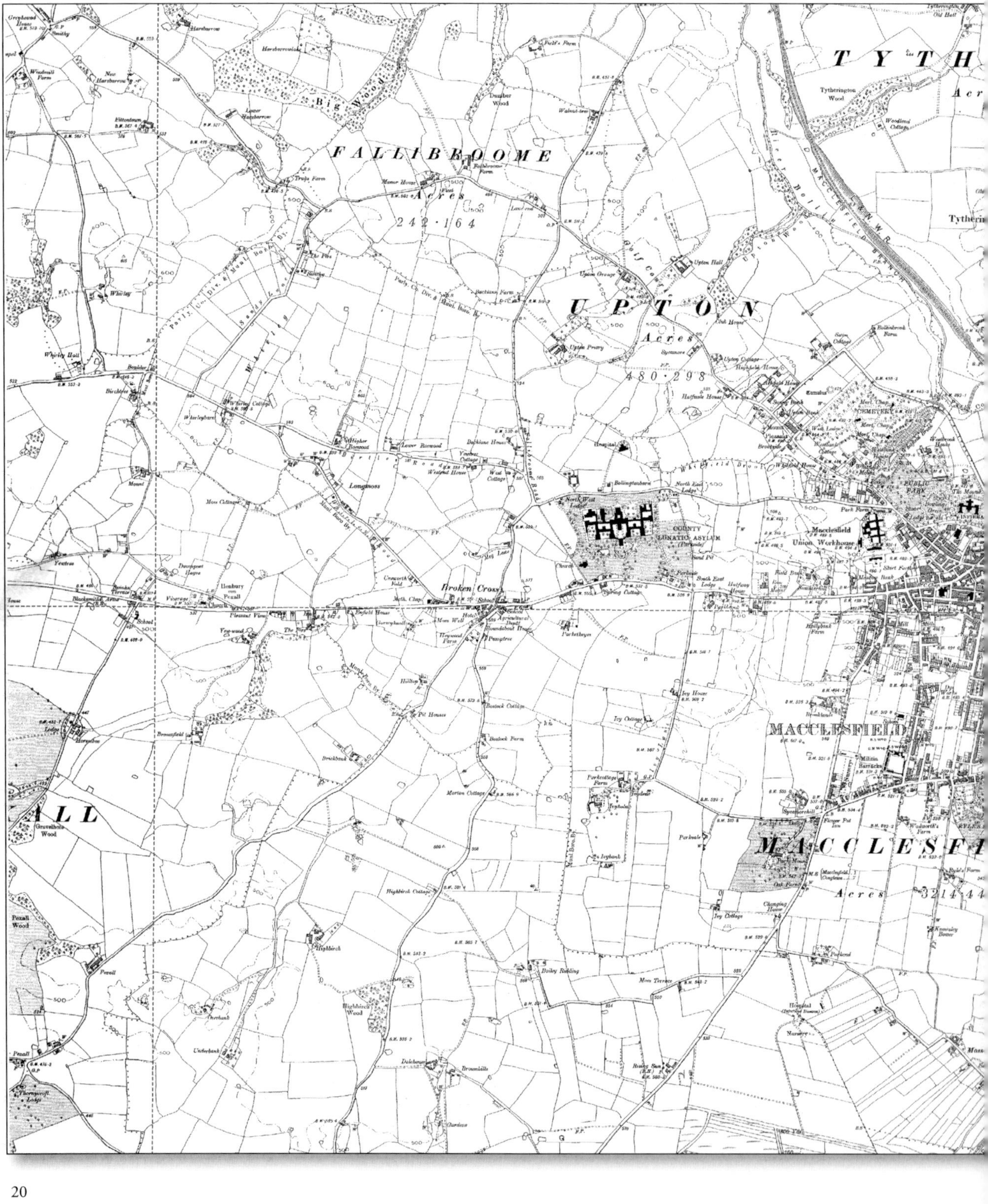

Ordnance Survey Map

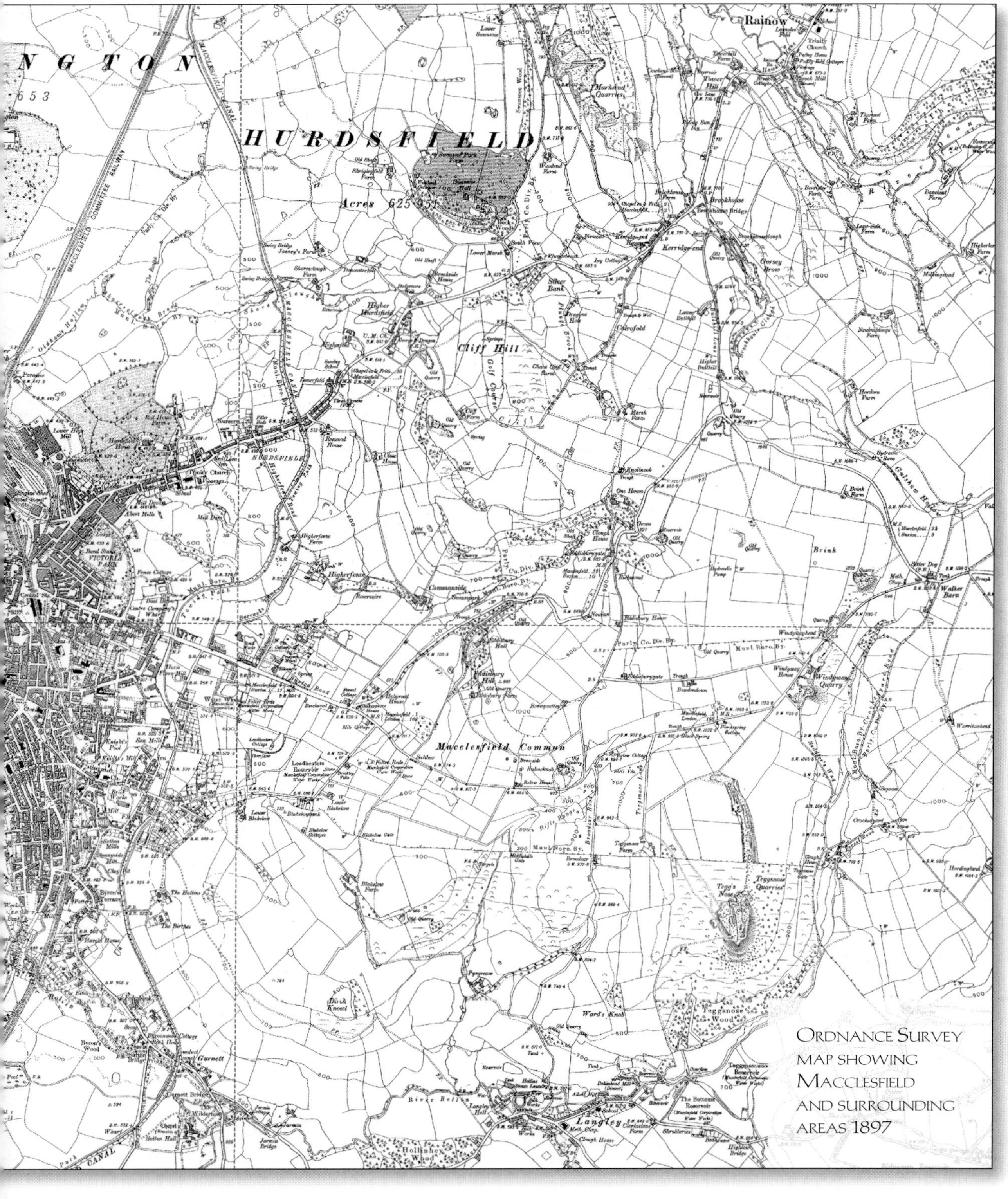

Ordnance Survey map showing Macclesfield and surrounding areas 1897

THE MARKET PLACE

The Market Place is the hub of the town. From here roads radiate north, south, west, and - after negotiating the Bollin valley - east. Here is the old church, the Town Hall, and several pubs. Today, after years of tyranny by traffic, the marketplace is pedestrianised, with beautiful stone setts instead of tarmac, but the market itself remains banished.

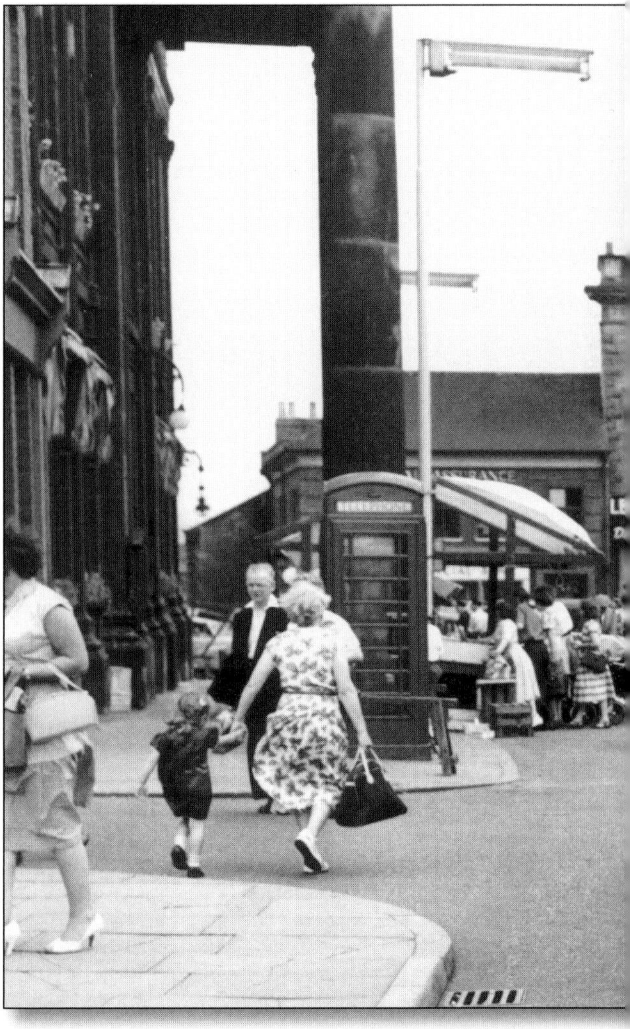

Set back a little behind railings and giving glimpses of the hills beyond is the old church of Macclesfield, St Michael's. It was founded by Queen Eleanor of Castile in 1278; she was so beloved of her warrior husband Edward I that he marked all the resting places of her funeral procession with a beautiful stone cross. It is very unusual to see two towers on a parish church. The big one is the bell tower, with no less than twelve bells which sound magnificent in full peal. It was built by the same master mason as the towers at Wybunbury and Tarvin, and perhaps Prestbury as well. The little tower is actually a house attached to the Savage chapel, which was built in 1505. It has fireplaces and a chimney and two little squints, so that the service can be followed both in the chapel and in the main church.

The body of the church has been rebuilt at least twice. Eleanor's church was replaced by a big Georgian preaching house in 1740, and that in turn disappeared right at the end of the 19th century to be replaced by the church we see today. The foundation stone of the new nave is dated 10 October 1898, and the rebuilt church was rededicated on 24 April 1901. 'Nave and aisles rebuilt, chancel largely altered, chapels and tower thoroughly restored' says the brass plate, 'architect Sir A Blomfield'. So the 1740 church must actually have been in the process of demolition at the time of Frith's first visit in 1897. It must have been an astonishing sight. While the church was out of action a 'tin tabernacle' was built in King Edward Street. Little can be discerned now of the first church, although we know it had a tall spire. The width of its nave, which was in line with the tower, is shown by the stumps of the two arcades, each with a carved head - are they Edward I and Eleanor? However, an exceptionally fine series of carved effigies of the Savage family has been preserved. Of the Georgian church we have the elegant font, the brass chandeliers, and the churchyard railings. I have never seen a photograph of its interior; it had galleries, classical columns and box pews. Presiding over the Market Place is the Town Hall, with its solemn columns facing south and west (M2018 pages 28-29). The churchyard side is the original one, complete with a platform under the portico for announcing election results. It was designed in 1823 by Francis Goodwin, who had recently built Manchester's first town hall on King Street. The Chestergate elevation was done by our own James Stevens (see page 60); he wanted to put a big stone cupola on top like the one at Bolton, which would have made a splendid landmark. From the marketplace we can take a stroll along Chestergate (42600 pages 32-33), a bustling and characterful street where there were once many family businesses and the shopkeepers lived above their shops. Chestergate is Georgian in aspect, but it is interesting to see bits of timber-framing appearing here and there in the alleyways and entries, revealing that the Georgian veneer is often only skin deep. Pedestrianisation, the first such scheme in Macclesfield, has

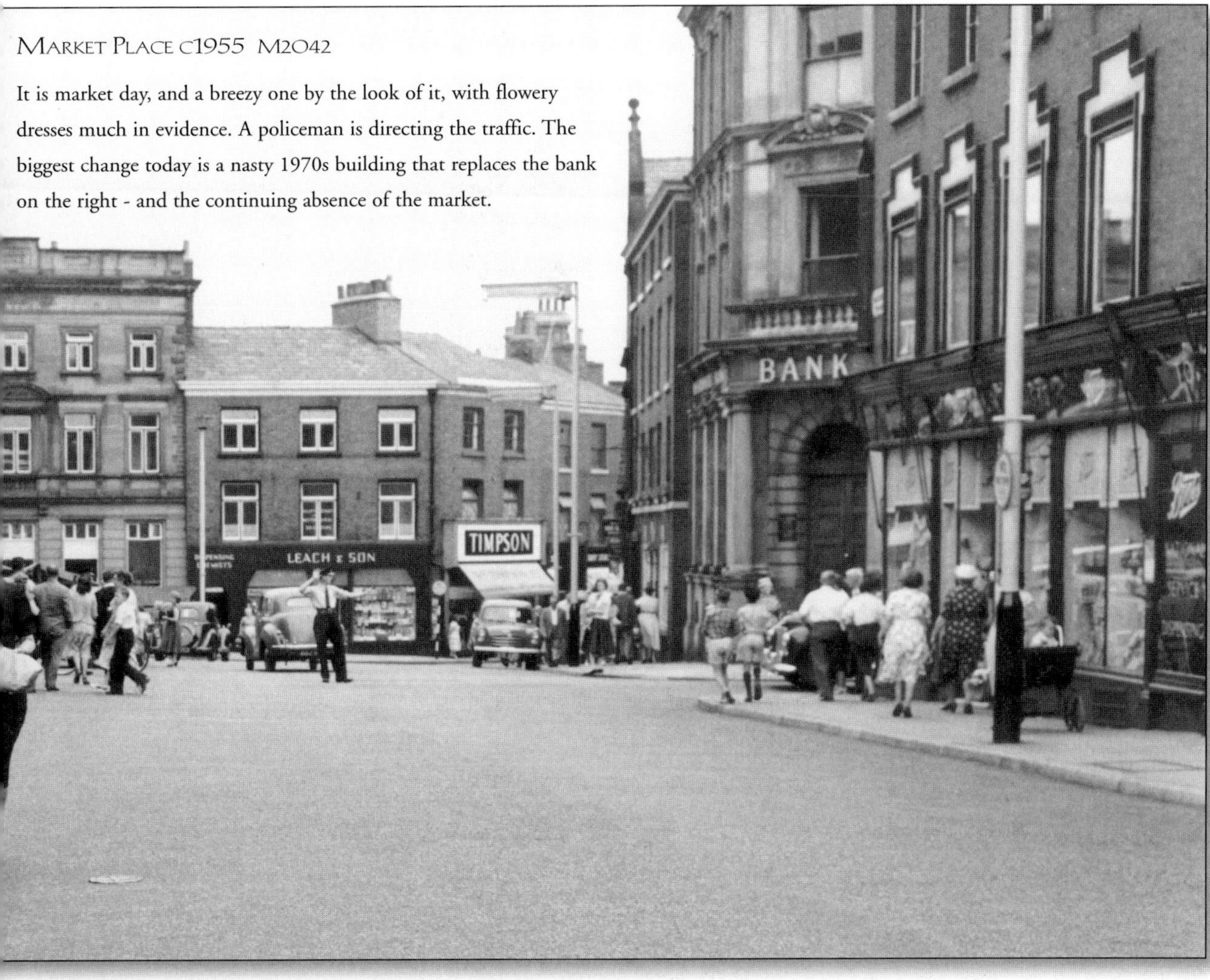

MARKET PLACE C1955 M2042

It is market day, and a breezy one by the look of it, with flowery dresses much in evidence. A policeman is directing the traffic. The biggest change today is a nasty 1970s building that replaces the bank on the right - and the continuing absence of the market.

allowed Chestergate to return to something like its 1898 aspect.The experimental pedestrianisation scheme was tried out in Chestergate in the summer of 1979. It took some getting used to. I have an amusing photograph showing the road empty of traffic, but all the pedestrians sticking to the pavement out of force of habit. However, the scheme was rated a success, and pedestrianisation for much of the day was made permanent - with the line between road and pavement blurred by resurfacing.

THE MARKET PLACE

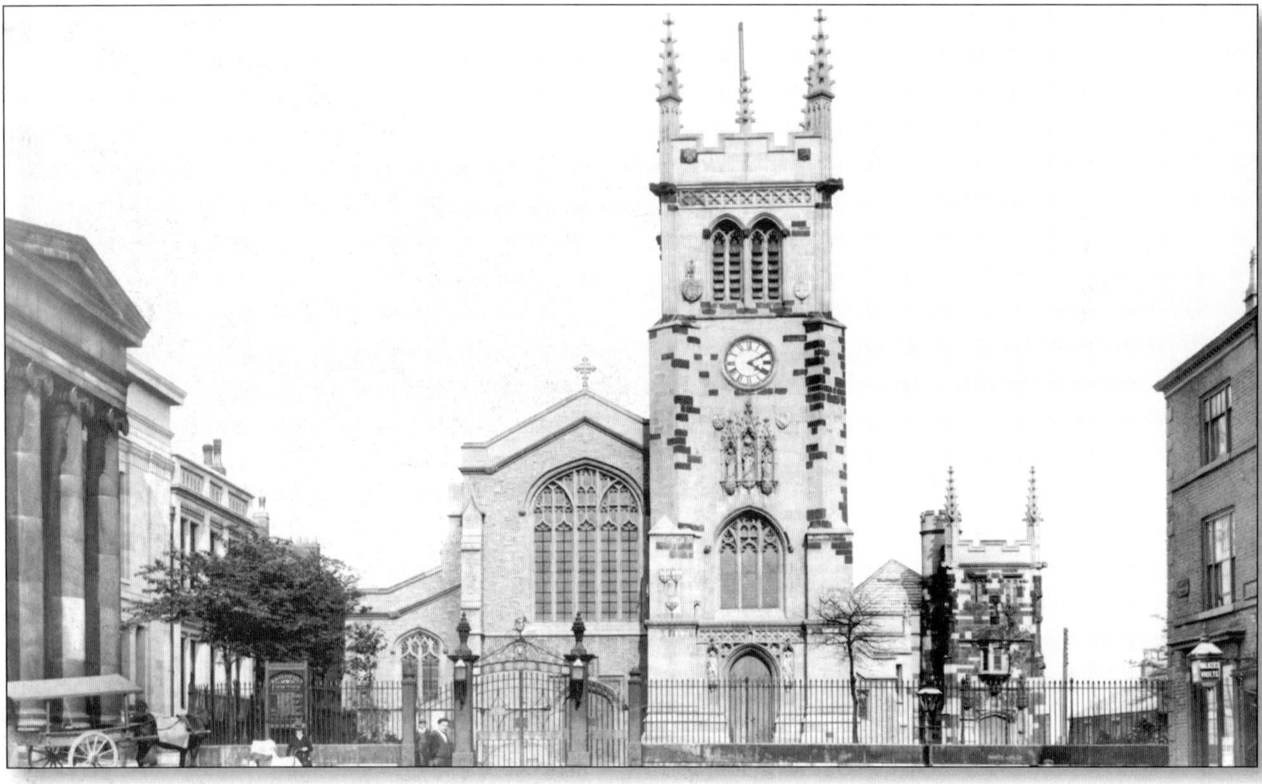

THE PARISH CHURCH 1903 49456

The old church had just undergone a radical rebuild, hence its strange piebald appearance. The west window of the new nave commemorates Queen Victoria, who had just died after the longest reign in British history. On the far right is Walker's Vaults, which was closed just three years later.

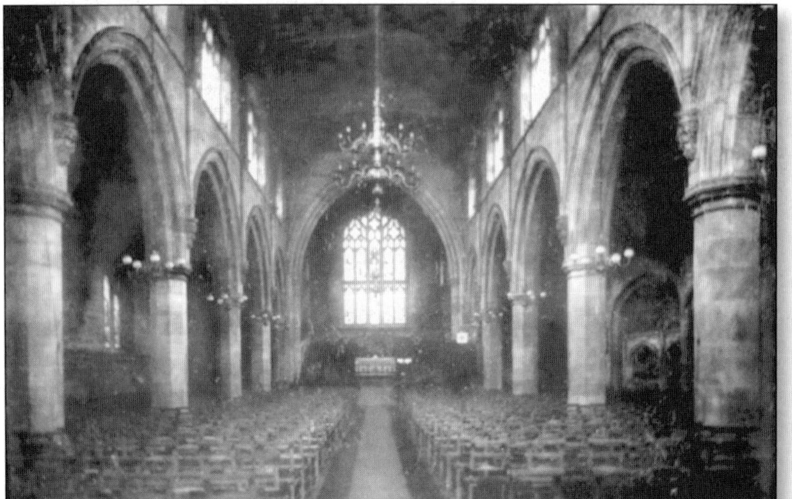

THE PARISH CHURCH, THE INTERIOR 1903 49458

The nave is by Blomfield, and would have been brand new when this photograph was taken. The chancel and east window were built a few years earlier and are by James Stevens. The fine chandeliers, still lit on special occasions, are Georgian.

THE MARKET PLACE

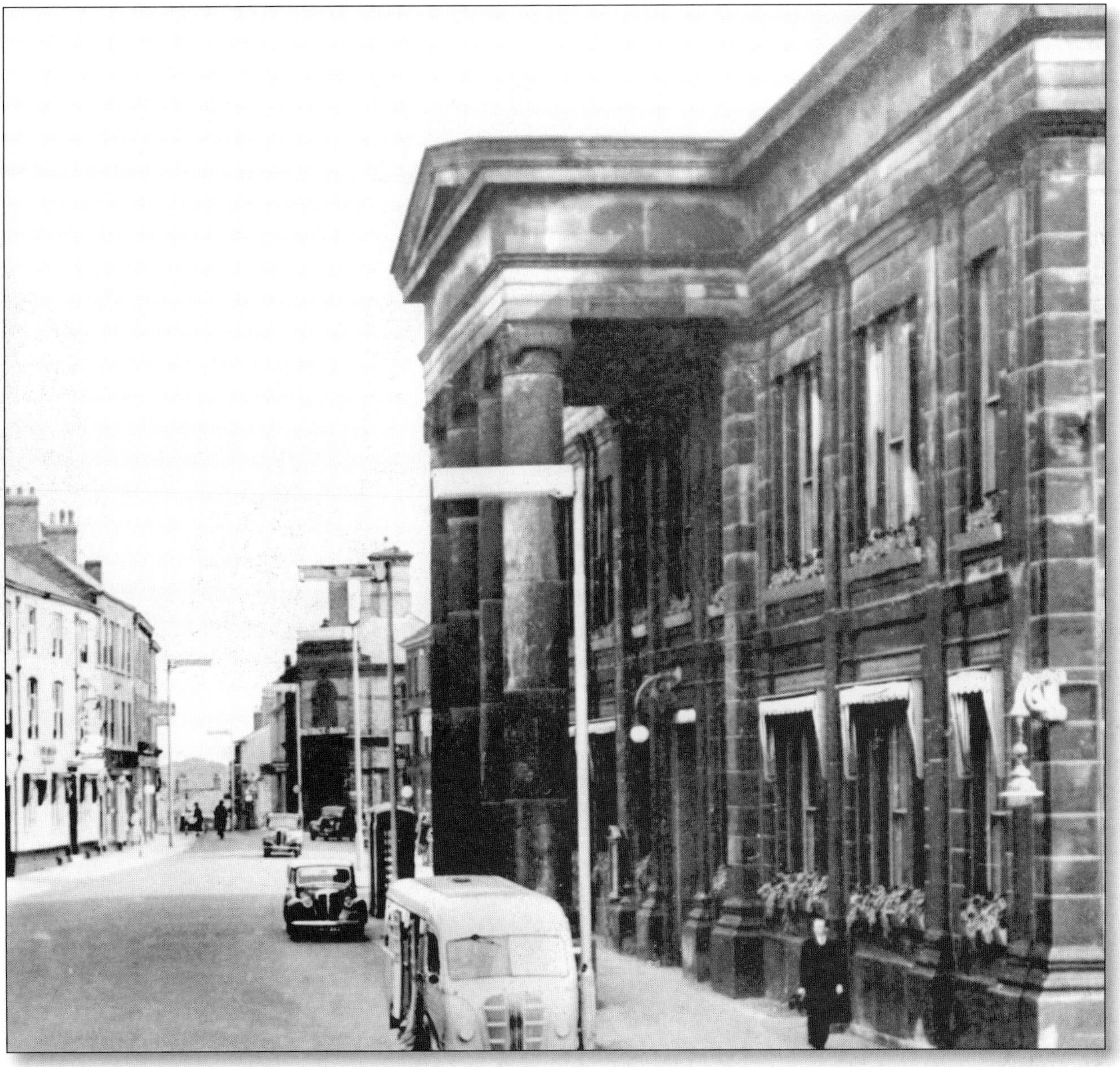

MARKET PLACE c1955 M2018

We can see how black the stonework was, apart from some replacement stones. Note the gas lamp still in place on the near corner.

COUNTY MAP

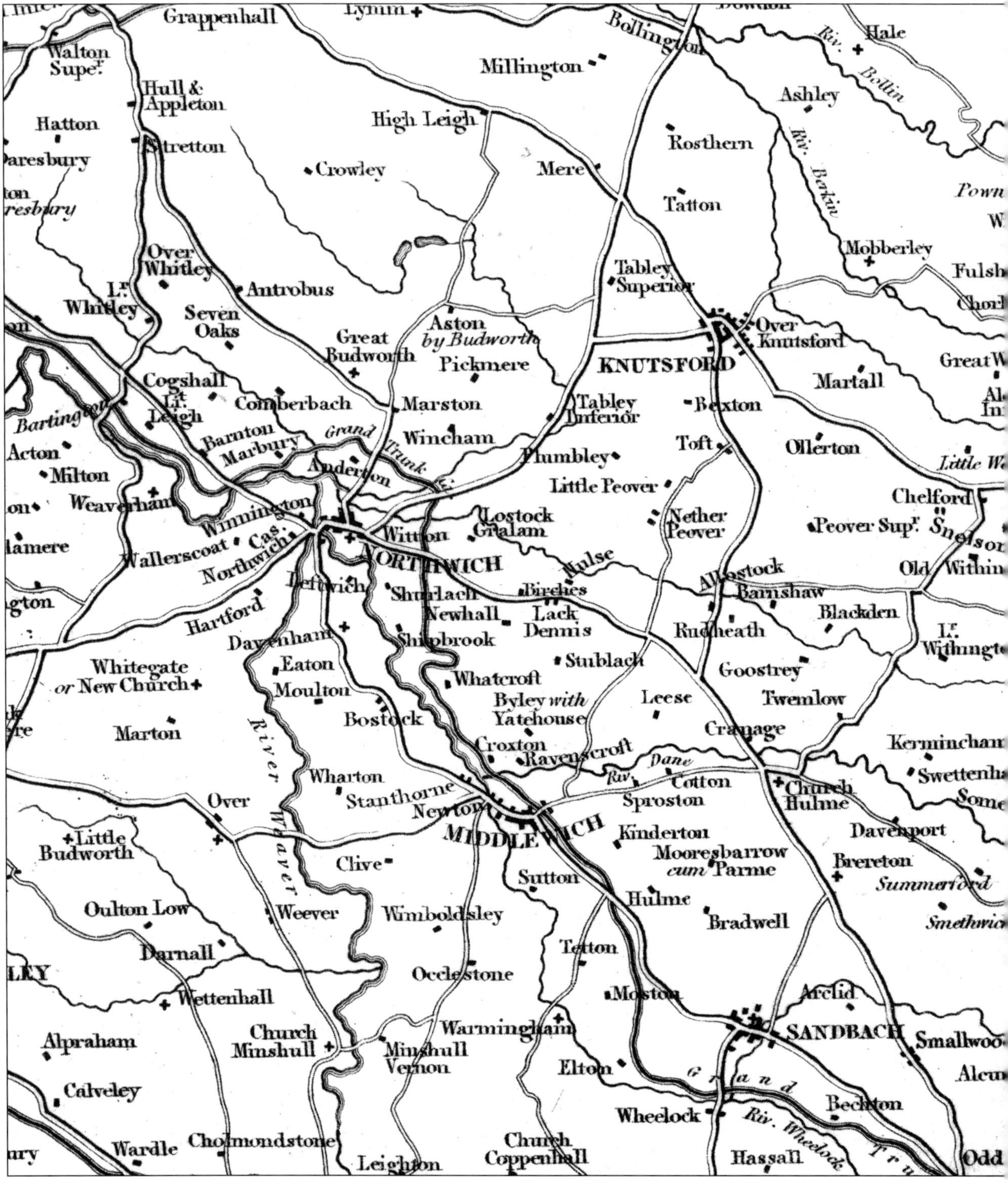
Grappenhall
Lymm
Bollington
Hale
Riv. Bollin
Walton Supe.r
Millington
Ashley
Hull & Appleton
Hatton
High Leigh
Rosthern
Stretton
Daresbury
Crowley
Mere
Riv. Birkin
Tatton
Town
Over Whitley
Mobberley
Lt. Whitley
Antrobus
Tabley Superior
Seven Oaks
Aston by Budworth
Over Knutsford
Great Budworth
Pickmere
KNUTSFORD
Martall
Cogshall
Lt. Leigh
Comberbach
Marston
Tabley Inferior
Bexton
Bartington
Grand Trunk
Barnton
Marbury
Wincham
Toft
Ollerton
Acton
Milton
Anderton
Plumbley
Little Peover
Chelford
Weaverham
Winnington
Lostock Gralam
Nether Peover
Peover Sup.r
Witton
Wallerscoat
Cas.
Northwich
NORTHWICH
Hulse
Allostock
Old Withington
Deftwich
Shurlach
Birches
Barnshaw
Blackden
Newhall
Lack Dennis
Hartford
Rudheath
Lt. Withington
Davenham
Shipbrook
Stublach
Whitegate or New Church
Eaton
Goostrey
Whatcroft
Moulton
Byley with Yatehouse
Leese
Twemlow
River Weaver
Bostock
Marton
Cranage
Croxton
Kermincham
Ravenscroft
Riv. Dane
Swettenham
Wharton
Cotton
Stanthorne
Church Hulme
Over
Sproston
Newton
MIDDLEWICH
Davenport
Little Budworth
Kinderton
Mooresbarrow cum Parme
Brereton
Clive
Summerford
Sutton
Oulton Low
Weever
Wimboldsley
Hulme
Bradwell
Smethwick
Tetton
Darnall
Occlestone
Arclid
Moston
Wettenhall
Warmingham
SANDBACH
Smallwood
Church Minshull
Alpraham
Minshull Vernon
Elton
Grand Trunk
Calveley
Bechton
Wheelock
Riv. Wheelock
Wardle
Cholmondstone
Church Coppenhall
Leighton
Hassall
Odd

COUNTY MAP

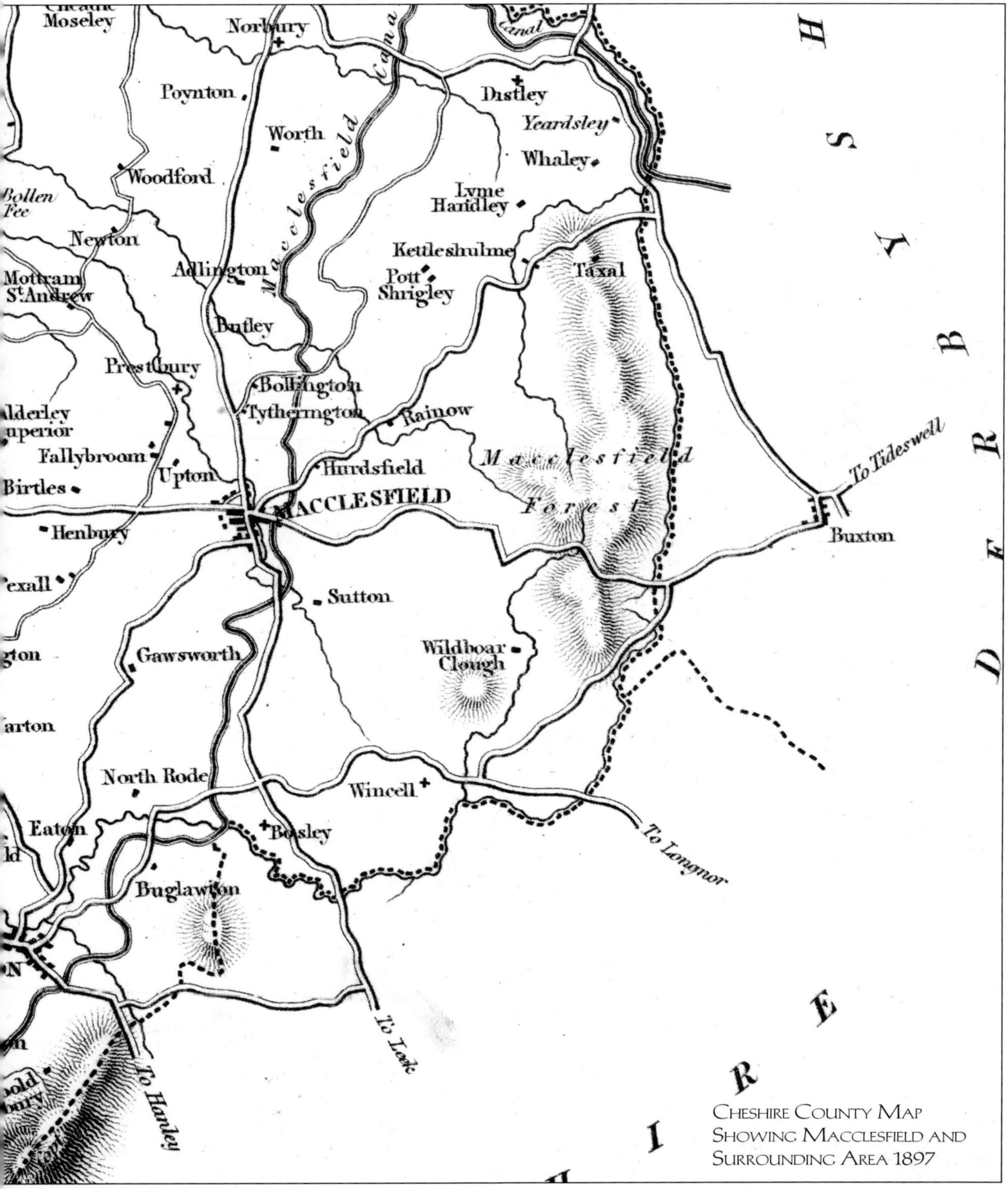

Cheshire County Map
Showing Macclesfield and
Surrounding Area 1897

THE MARKET PLACE

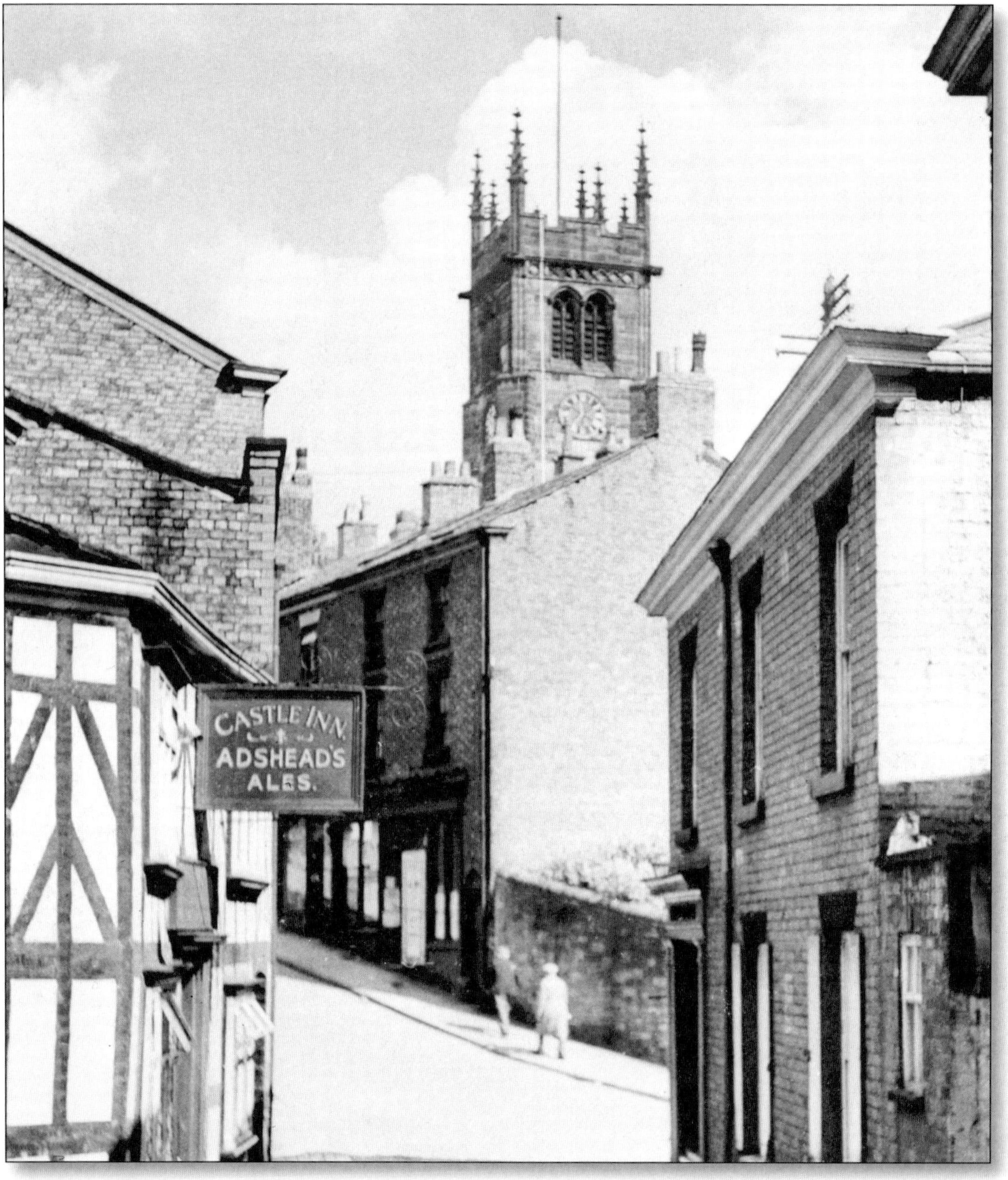

CHURCHWALLGATE C1955 M2003

The Castle Inn was described in an advertisement of 1911 as 'Cosy, Comfortable and Central', which would still be a good description. Hereabouts, as the pub's name tells us, stood the 'castle', or Great Place of Macclesfield. The photographer stood with his back to its outer wall. In reality it was a stone manor house. The final remains were demolished in 1933; a few carved stones were kept, and much battered, are preserved in the Town Hall courtyard.

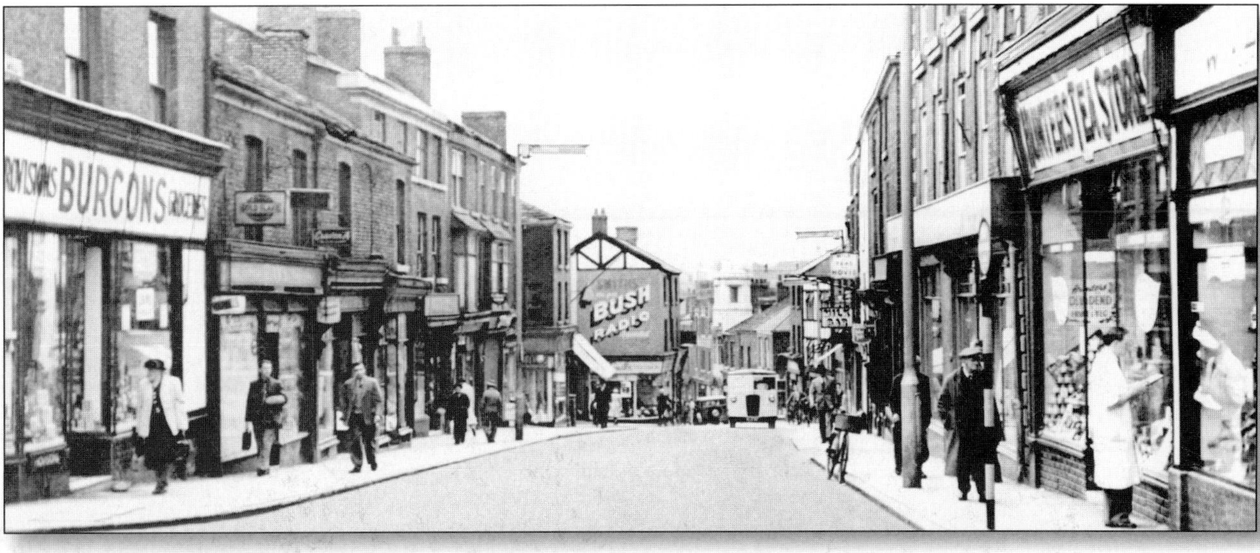

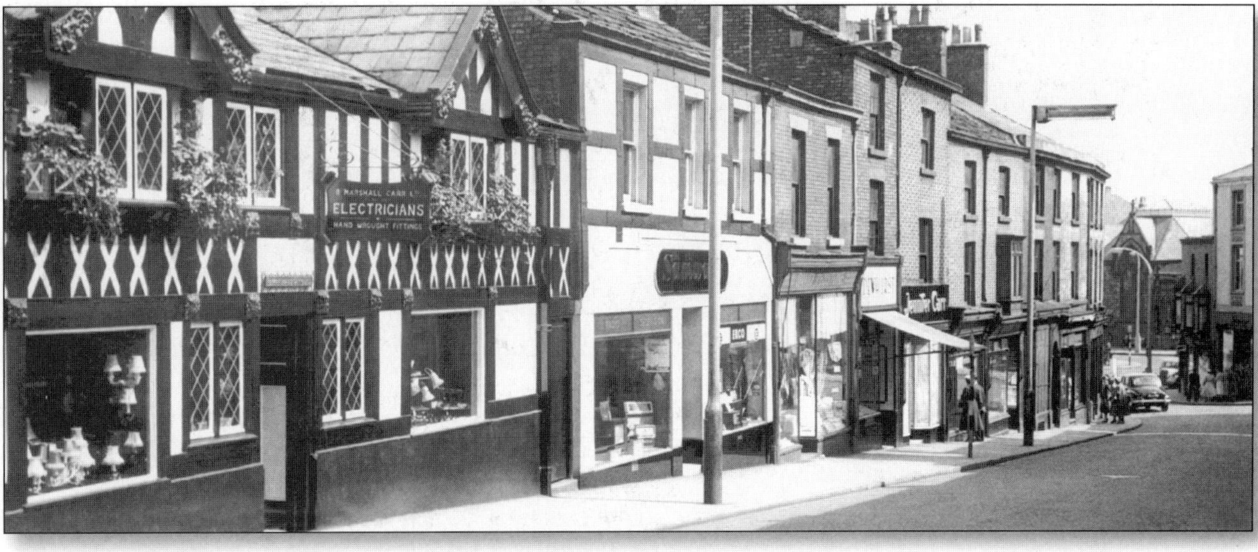

TOP: MILL STREET C1955 M2016

The town may have been dingy in 1955, but you could buy anything you wanted. The little white tower of the late lamented Majestic Cinema of 1922 rises in the middle distance.

BOTTOM: MILL STREET C1955 M2027

More or less opposite the Majestic stands this little black-and-white building, originally the Pig and Whistle, then for many years Marshall Carr's, the electricians. It is a genuinely old building, but the timber framing is entirely bogus. Recently it reverted, but unsuccessfully, to being the Pig and Whistle again.

THE MARKET PLACE

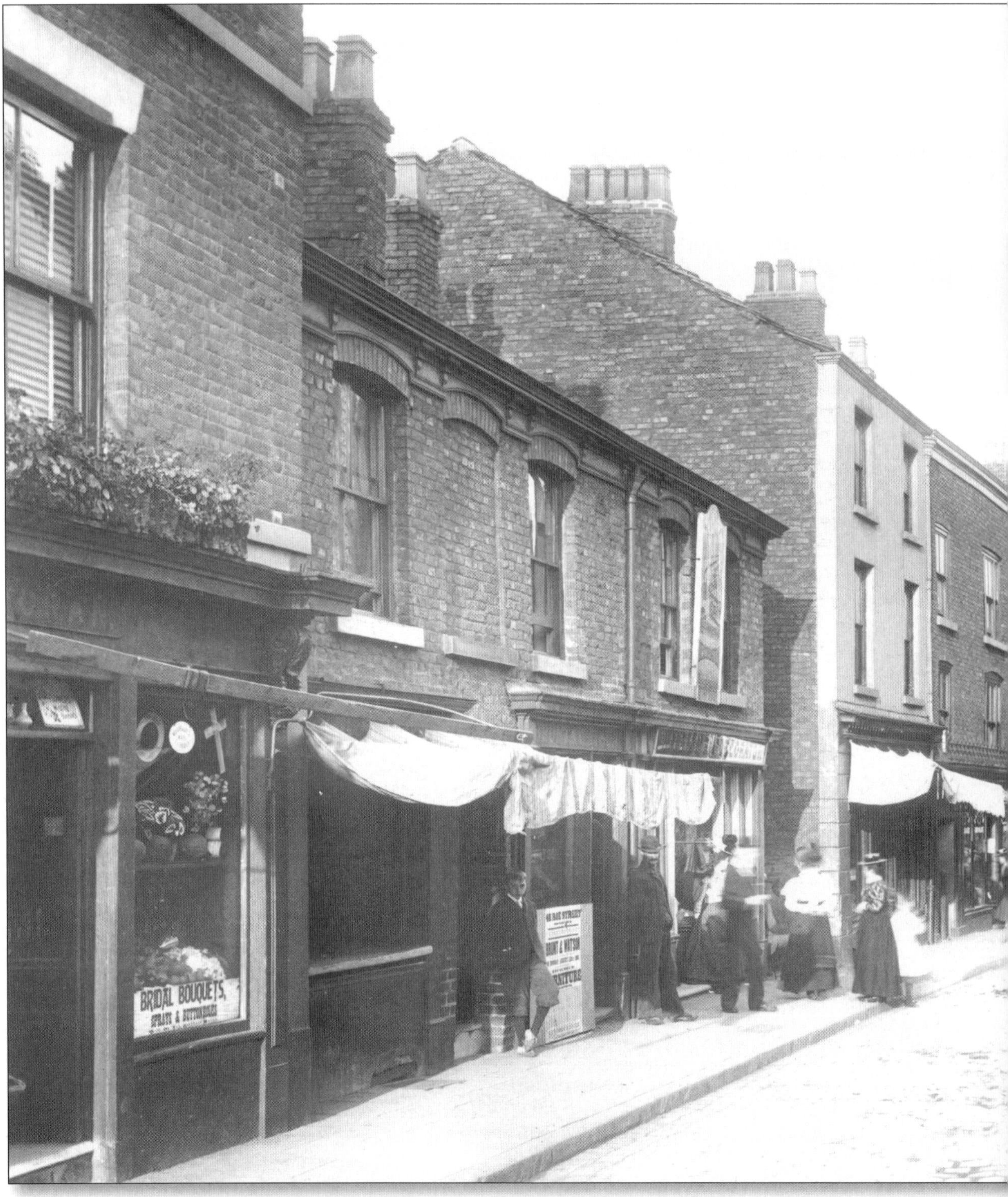

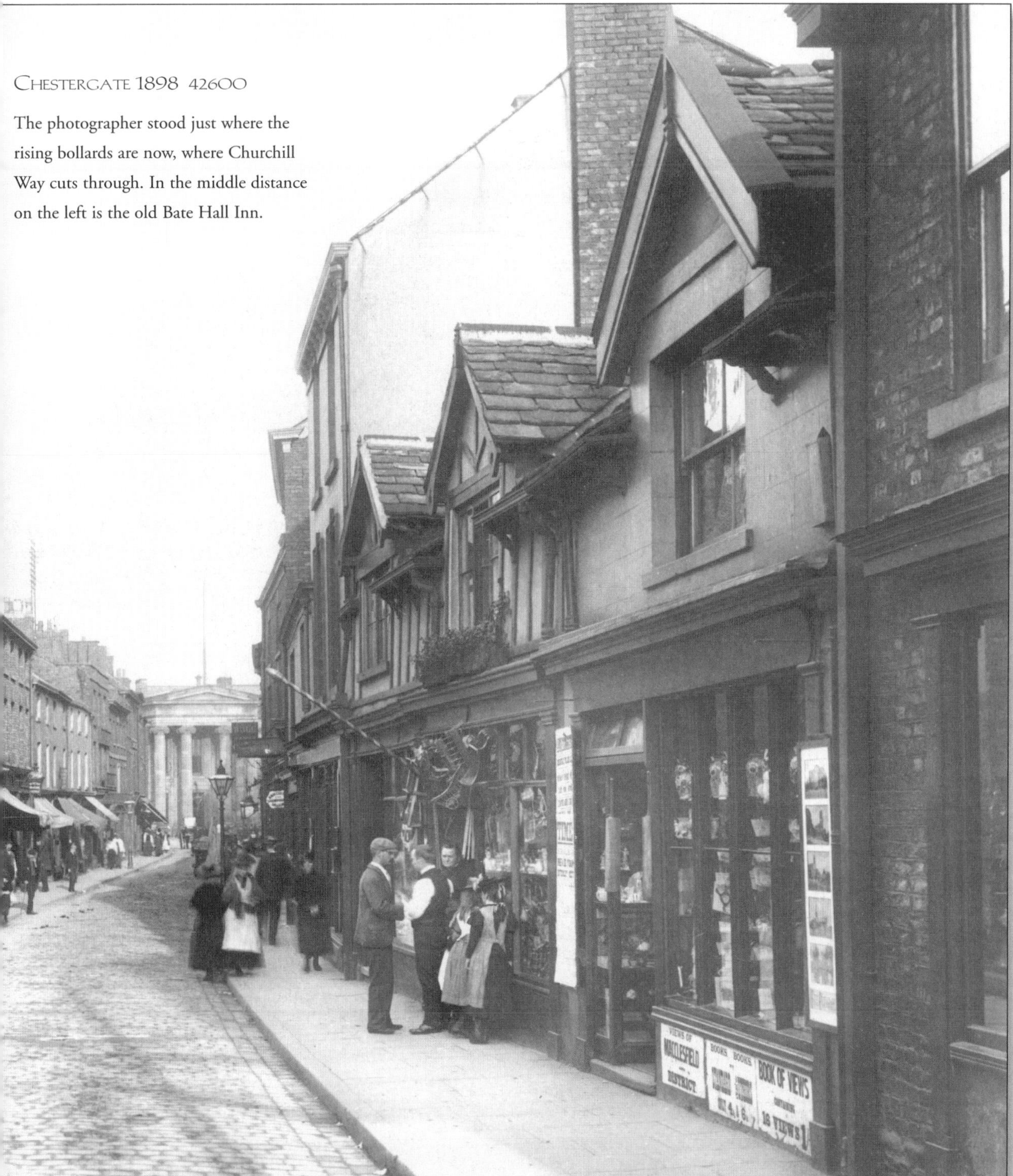

CHESTERGATE 1898 42600

The photographer stood just where the rising bollards are now, where Churchill Way cuts through. In the middle distance on the left is the old Bate Hall Inn.

PARK GREEN

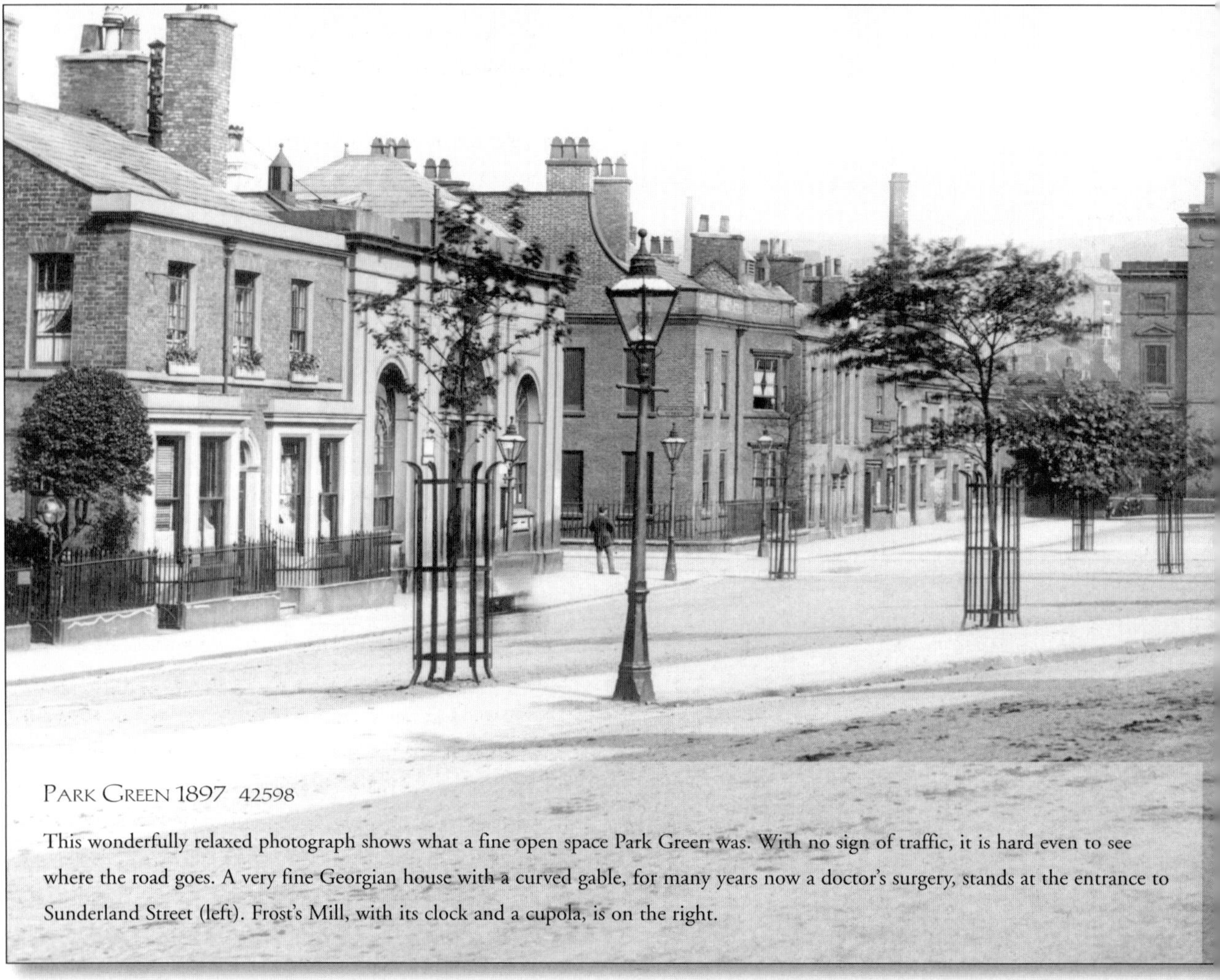

PARK GREEN 1897 42598

This wonderfully relaxed photograph shows what a fine open space Park Green was. With no sign of traffic, it is hard even to see where the road goes. A very fine Georgian house with a curved gable, for many years now a doctor's surgery, stands at the entrance to Sunderland Street (left). Frost's Mill, with its clock and a cupola, is on the right.

Originally, Park Green must have been a big grassy green sloping gently down to the Bollin, which is largely hidden today, and bordering on to the great park or hunting forest that stretched out towards Gawsworth. We can imagine that it was a good place for gatherings and fairs and bucolic games. At the time of Frith's first visits it was still a pleasant wide open space, good for promenading and passing the time of day, with small trees dotted about, fine buildings around it and a splendid iron fountain as a focus (40442 page 39).

Today Park Green is little more than a complicated road junction. The sense of a single space has been whittled away by all the clutter associated with roads and by the piecemeal development in the odd-shaped spaces left over. The fountain went for scrap in the Second World War. Apparently its twin still exists in the Scottish town of Strathpeffer, so it would be perfectly possible to reinstate it. In fact it would be possible to bring back all the dignity and sense of place to this neglected asset, as Bristol has proved with its astonishing reinstatement of Queen Square.Compare photographs 40442 (page 39) and 49465 (page 38), and spot the difference between them! The delightful centrepiece of Park Green was the cast iron fountain presented by James Kershaw. It was one of the chief landmarks of the town, and gave Park Green an identity which it grievously lacks today. The Congregational Chapel, now the United

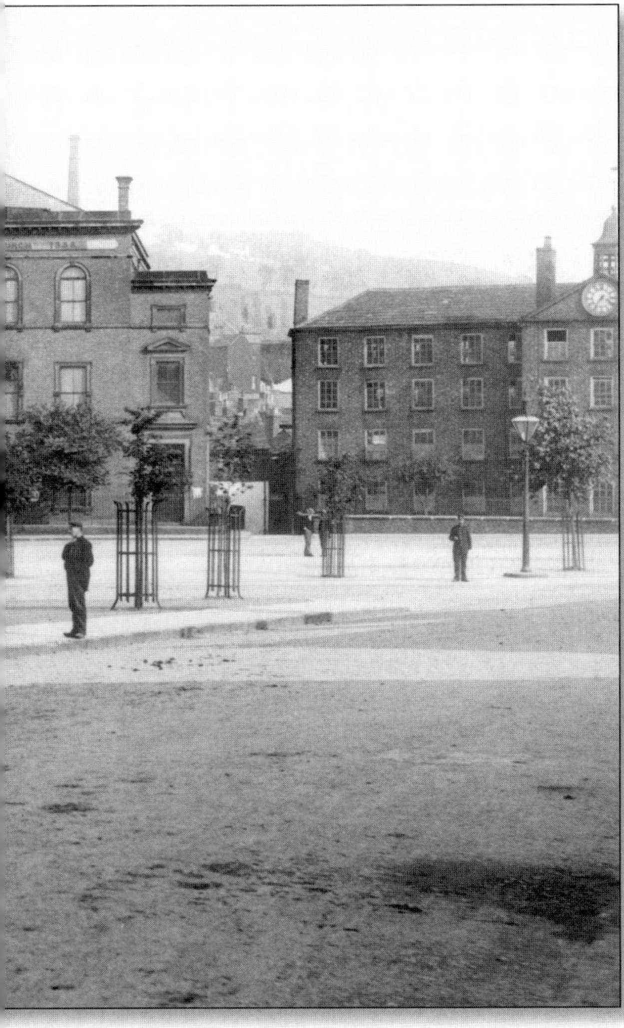

Reformed Church, was built in 1877 to replace the old Calvinist chapel behind it in Towneley Street, which still stands. The powerful Doric-columned Savings Bank was built in 1818 - it certainly looks as though your savings would be safe there! Apart from changing fashions in gas lamps, the difference between the pictures is that the Manchester and Liverpool District Bank has built a branch here in place of Curphey's removals office. It was a charming building, full of importance despite its diminutive size. The interior was colourfully tiled, and there was a coal fire to warm customers. Today a very dull 1980s block stands in its place.

Costing £5,410, the library (49466, page 38) and 10,000 books was the gift of Mr David Chadwick, who was the town's MP from 1868-80. It opened with great celebrations on 27 May 1876. On the right of 49466 we see the School of Art of 1879 (it says 1877 over the door); on the left is the Technical School which was finished in 1898, so it was brand new when this photograph was taken. Compare this picture with 40451 on page 64. Today the library, unfortunately shorn of all its rooftop extravagances which create such a good skyline, is the Register Office.

Near Park Green is Roe Street, named after Charles Roe, and the Big Sunday School (40460, page 47), which is today's Heritage Centre. It certainly is big; since the demolition of Stockport's Sunday School, it is probably the largest in the country.

The Sunday School owes its origin to John Whitaker. When he was only 24, he started a non-denominational school run by volunteers in temporary premises in Pickford Street. That was in 1796. Within four weeks, they were overwhelmed with the number of children attending. At the end of the first year there were 582 on the roll, and by 1800 there were 1,128. In 1812, with more than 2,000 children attending each week, the decision was made to erect the present building. A fine model was made, which still exists; it was probably trundled round the town on a barrow to raise funds. The next year the foundation stone was laid amid general rejoicing, and the school opened in 1814. The first Superintendent was, of course, John Whitaker. Sad to say, he died in 1820 - he was only 48.

The Big Sunday School is a very unusual building: the lower floors are subdivided into rooms and corridors as one would expect, but the top two floors are in reality a single huge auditorium, complete even to a fine organ built by Samuel Renn and recently restored. The auditorium would be packed by the children attending; in the first year there were 2,451 children and 200 teachers. Some of the original iron and wood benches remain in the gallery, but today the main auditorium has been comfortably re-seated for concerts and other gatherings.

A short walk beyond will take us to Christchurch (42607 and 49462, pages 46-47). It is a great big brick box of a church with a tall gaunt tower, strong in its massing, standing in a large square churchyard. Construction started in May 1775 and the church was opened on Christmas Day the same year, an astonishing feat, and achieved without accident. The tower was built the following year.

PARK GREEN

Christchurch was constructed at the sole expense (which was near £8,000) of the entrepreneur industrialist Charles Roe. He built it for the saintly Rev David Simpson, who was in danger of being ejected from St Michael's because of his sympathy and friendship with the great John Wesley, the enthusiast and Methodist. Wesley visited Christchurch and preached to the multitudes from its towering pulpit on many occasions; although an Anglican church, it is indeed one of the shrines of Methodism.

Sad to say, Christchurch closed shortly after its bicentenary because it was considered unsuitable to modern worship. The ten bells in its tower still ring out on a Monday evening, although they sound rather muffled - they are now hung nearer the bottom than the top for safety reasons. The church is well cared for by the Churches Conservation Trust, and is open most days.

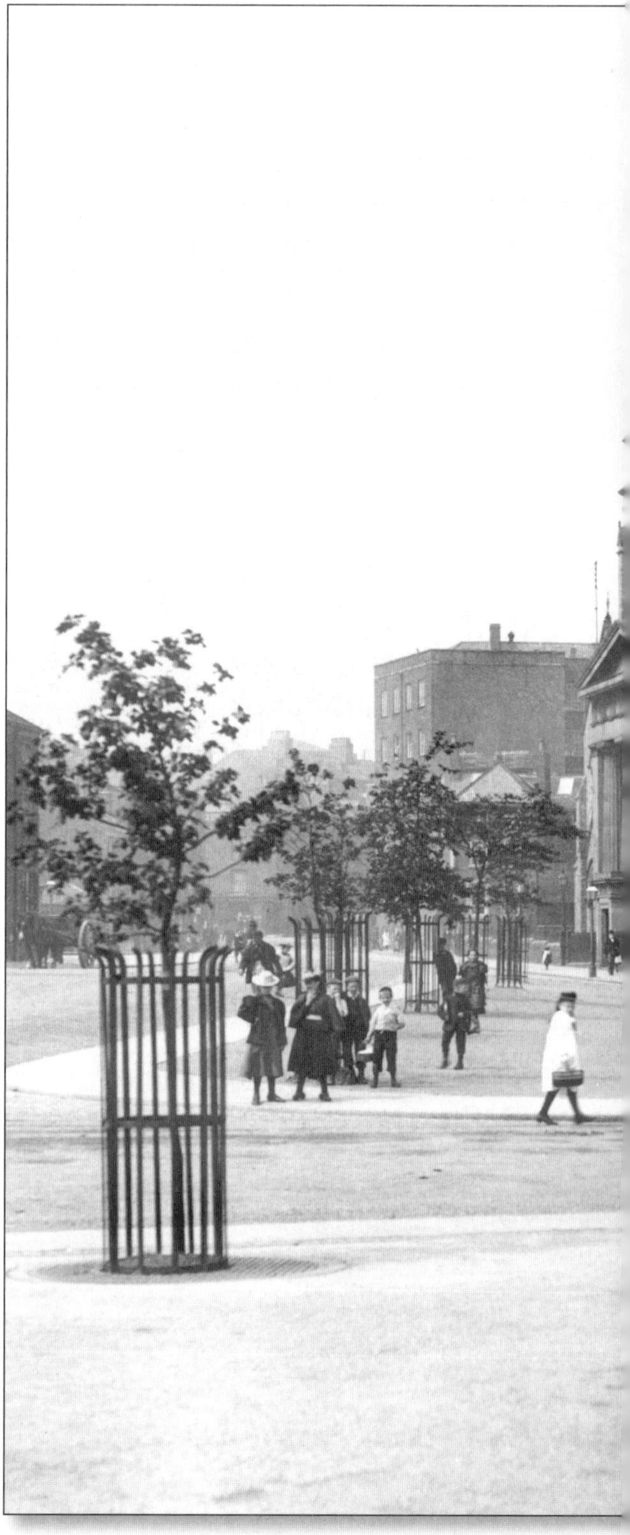

PARK GREEN 1897 42597

The photographer was standing in the same place as in 42598 (pages 34-35), but looking the other way. A few more people are about. The Post Office and the handsome house next to it are where the Co-op, or Equitable Provident Society, was to build its headquarters in 1933. Beyond the tower is Charles Roe's Depot Mill.

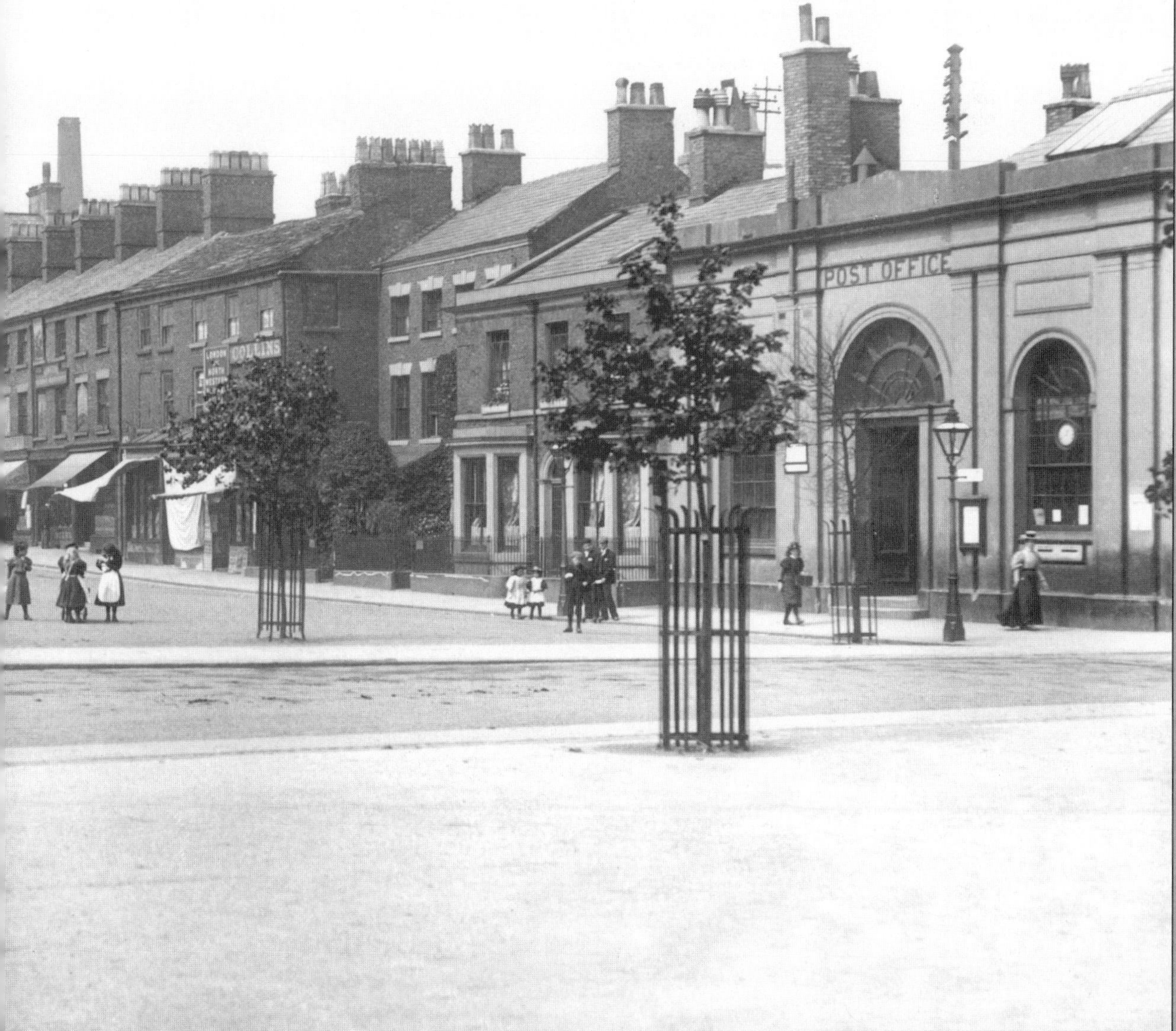

PARK GREEN

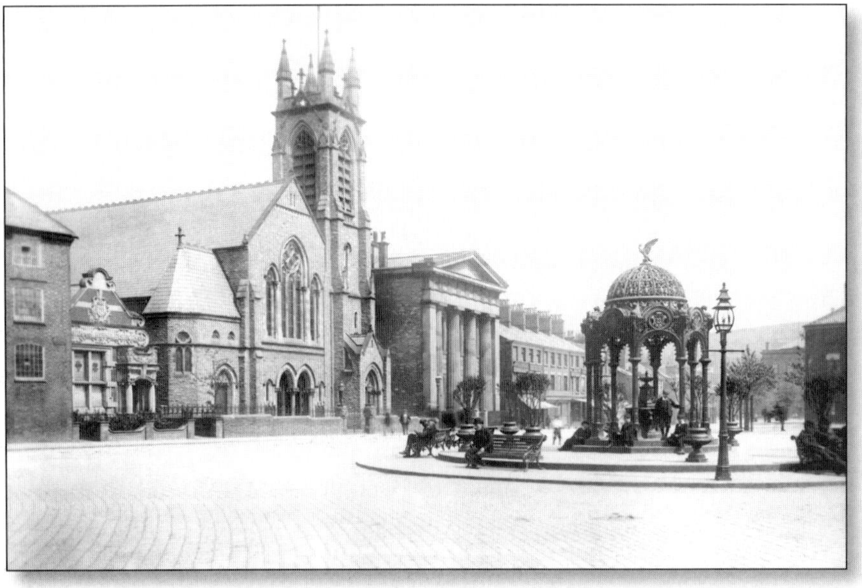

Above: Park Green 1903 49465

Below: The Free Library 1903 49466

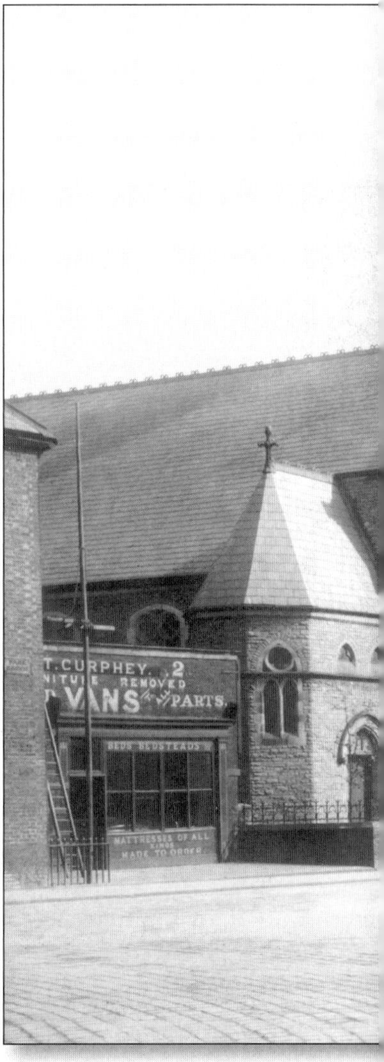

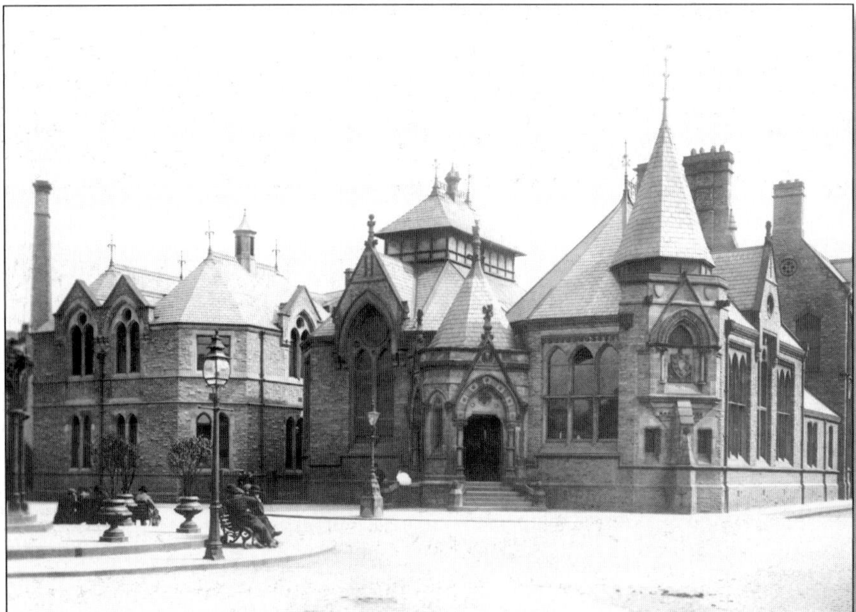

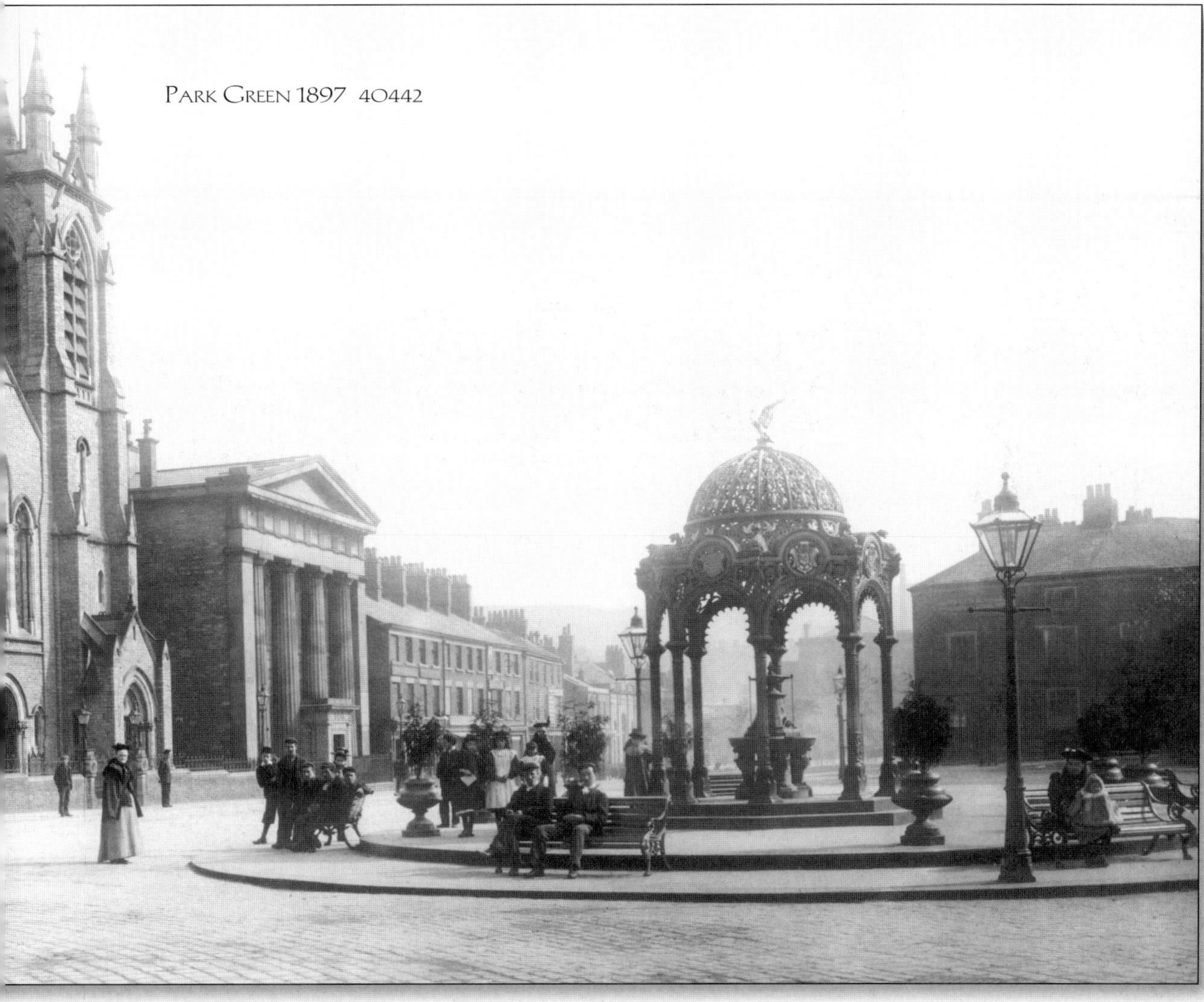

Park Green 1897 40442

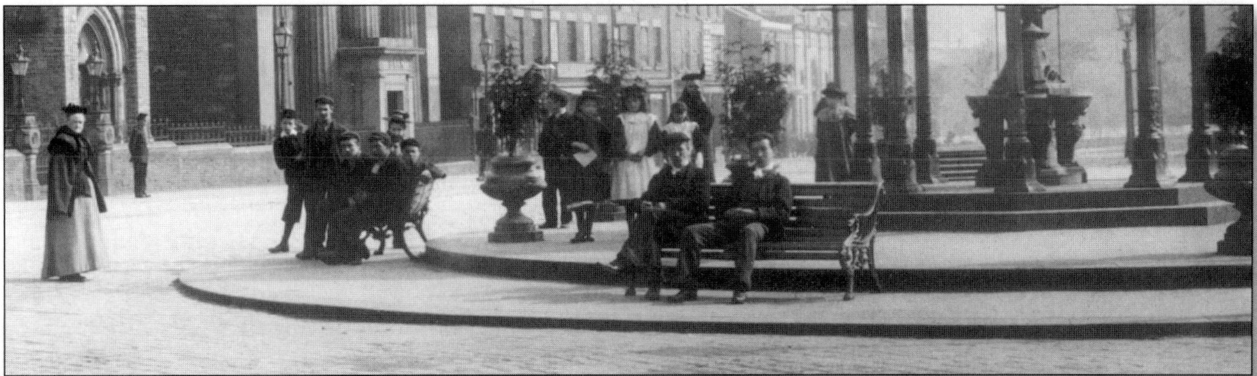

PARK GREEN

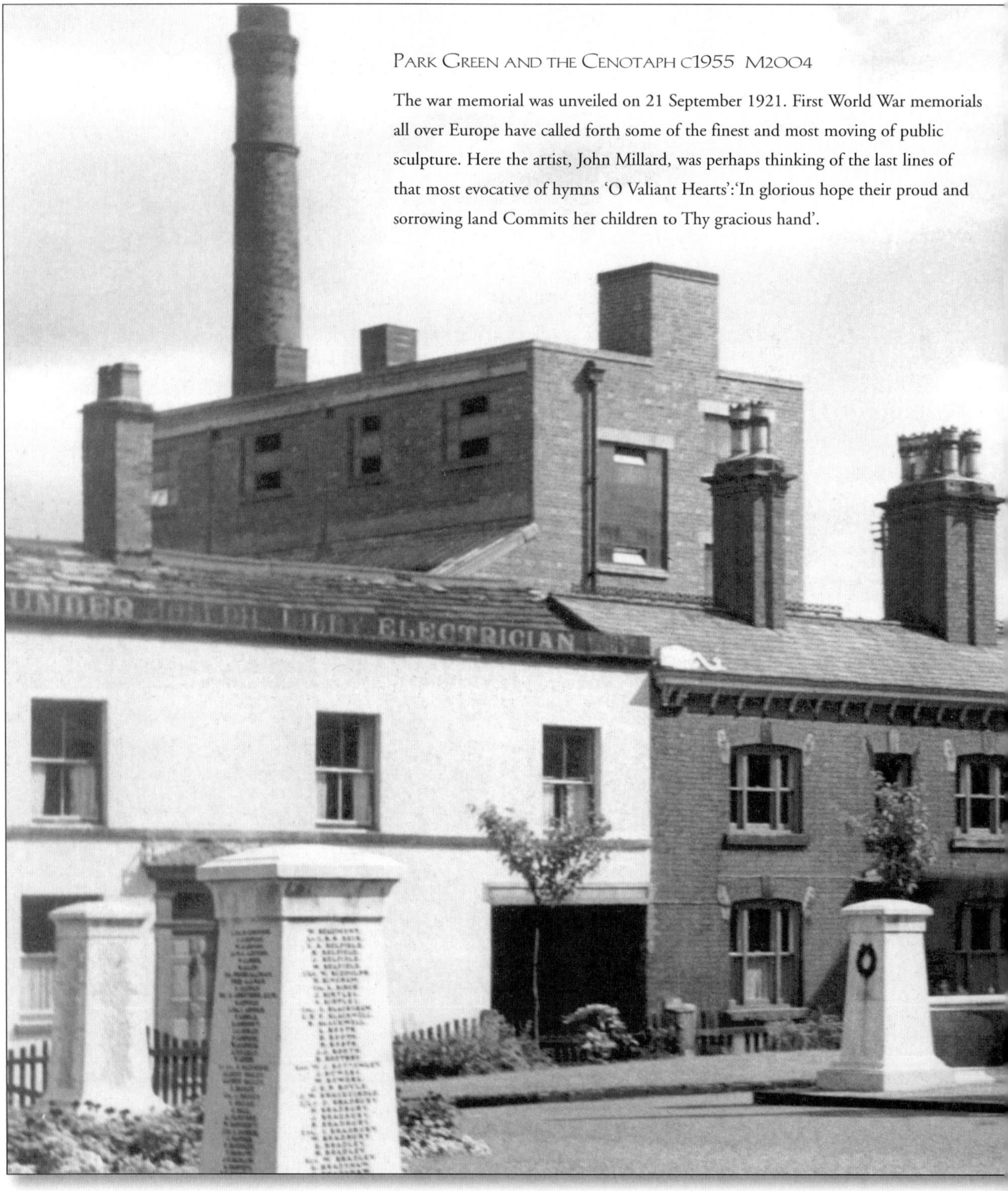

PARK GREEN AND THE CENOTAPH C1955 M2004

The war memorial was unveiled on 21 September 1921. First World War memorials all over Europe have called forth some of the finest and most moving of public sculpture. Here the artist, John Millard, was perhaps thinking of the last lines of that most evocative of hymns 'O Valiant Hearts':'In glorious hope their proud and sorrowing land Commits her children to Thy gracious hand'.

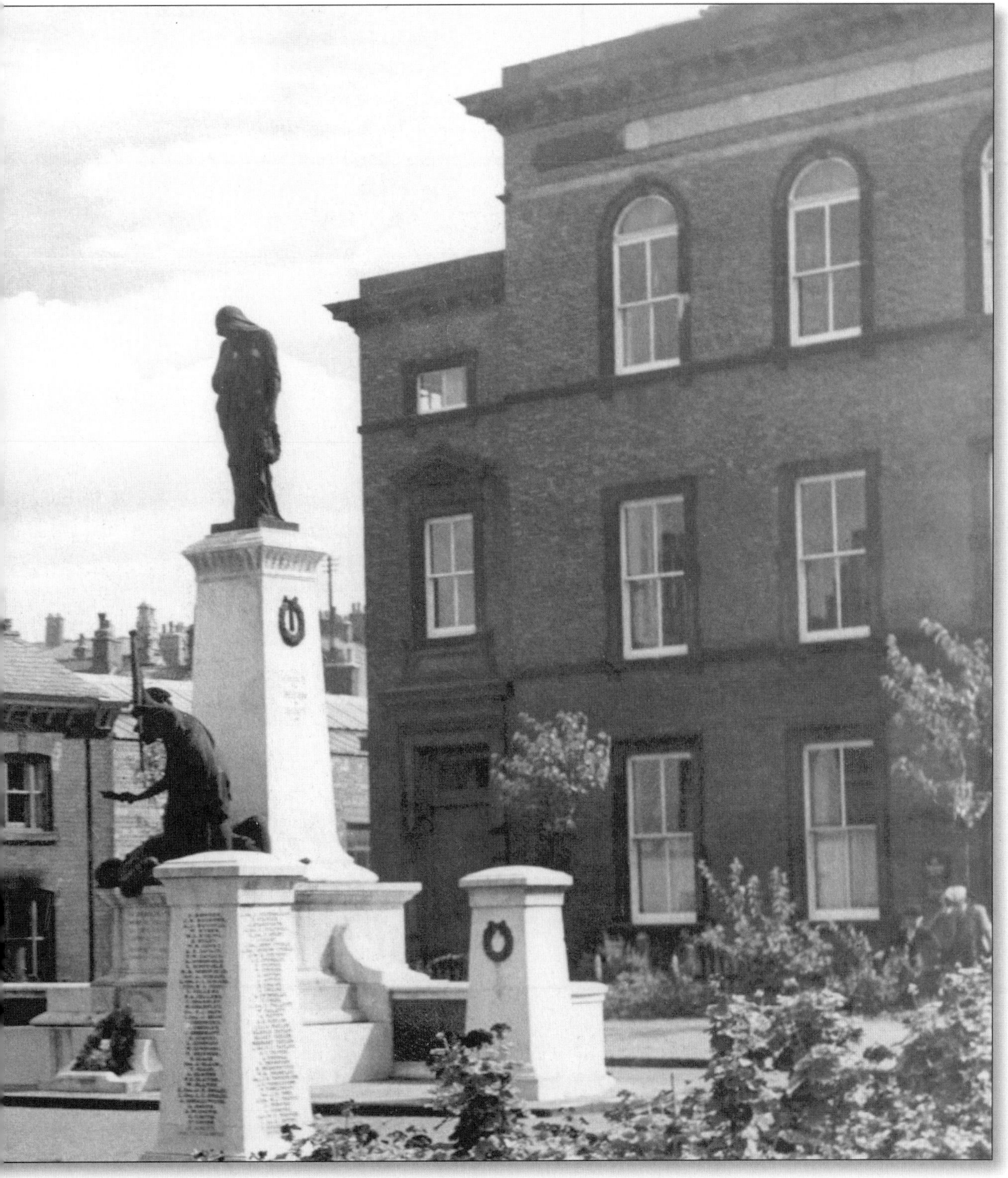

PARK GREEN

PARK GREEN AND THE CENOTAPH c1955 M2029

A smart Ford Prefect in green with white-wall tyres speeds though town. It is the only smart thing in the picture. Fifty years, and the advent of the motor car, have diminished Park Green as a recognisable place. On the skyline is St Paul's church, which is still with us, and a tall chimney, which has gone.

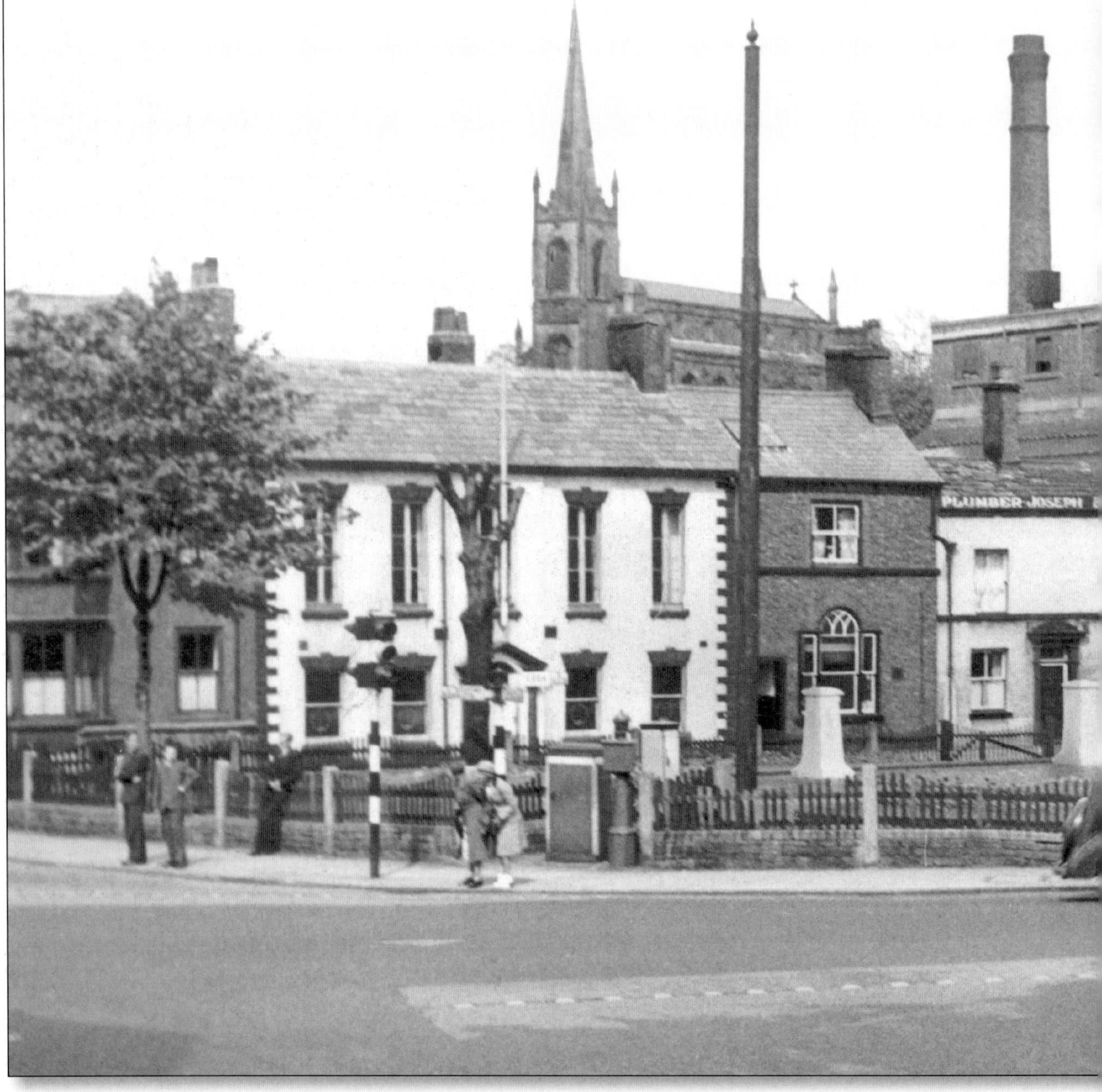

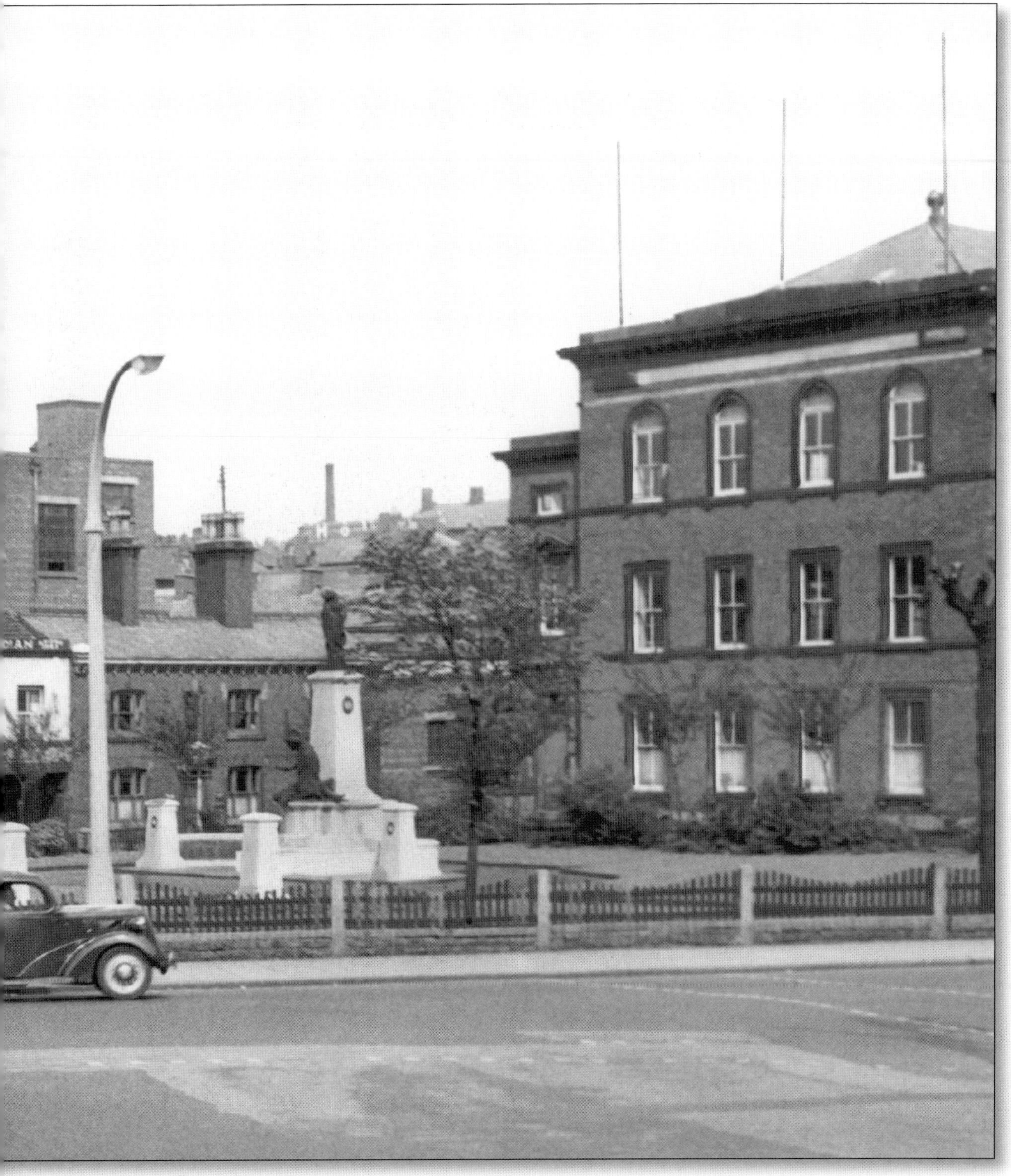
PAN

PARK GREEN

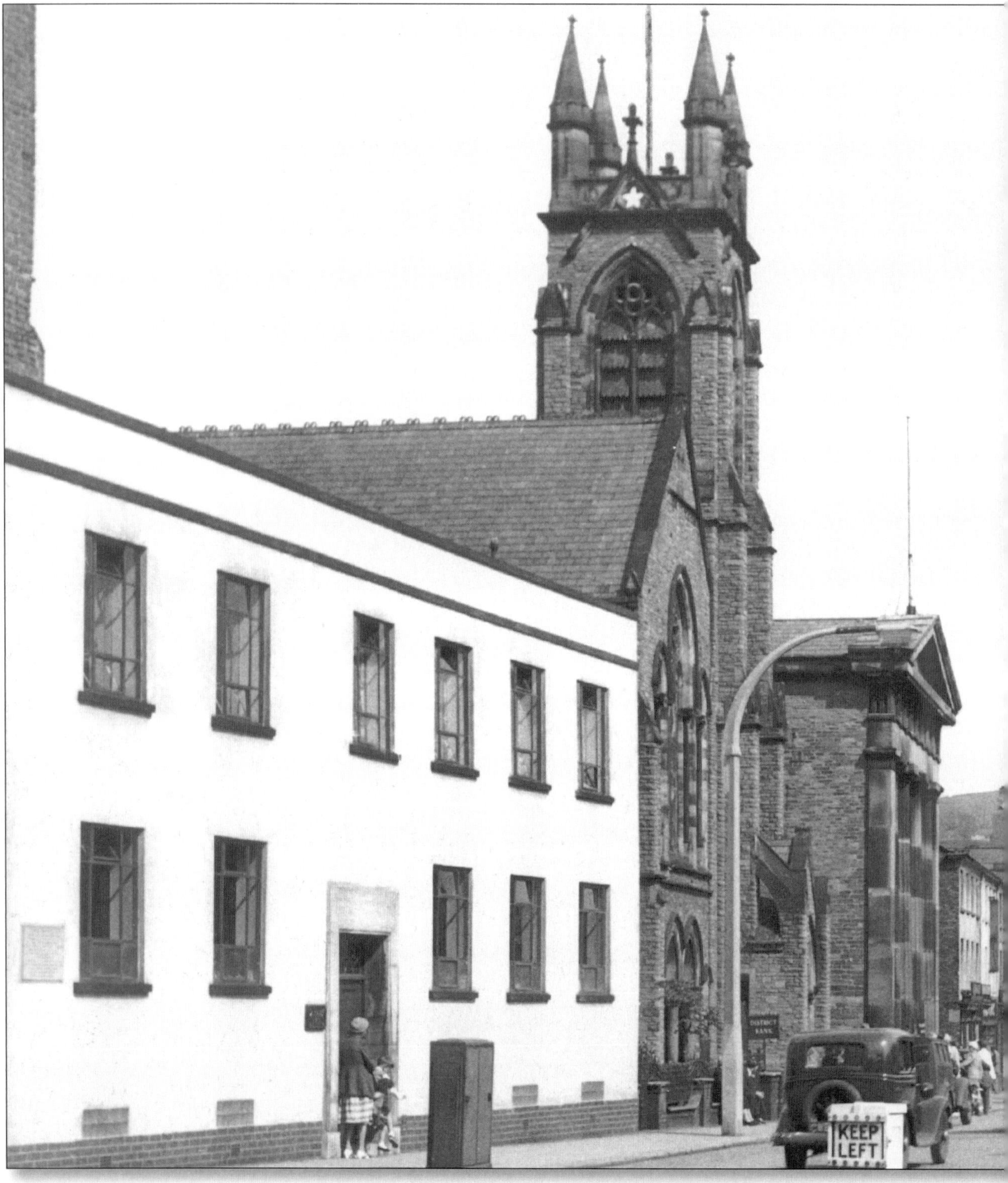

PARK GREEN c1955 M2028

Compared with 42598 (page 34), this telling photograph (M2028) shows once again how much damage the car has done to our towns - although I like the series 1 Landrover emerging on the right! The iron fountain has gone, and Frost's Mill has lost its cupola (centre right, in the distance). Depot Mill can just be seen behind the white building; the Dams Brook passes underneath at just this point; this would have provided the power, just as the Bollin behind Frost's Mill provided the power there. In the distance is the green hill of the Hollins. Perhaps the best feature of Macclesfield is that you can always lift up your eyes unto the hills.

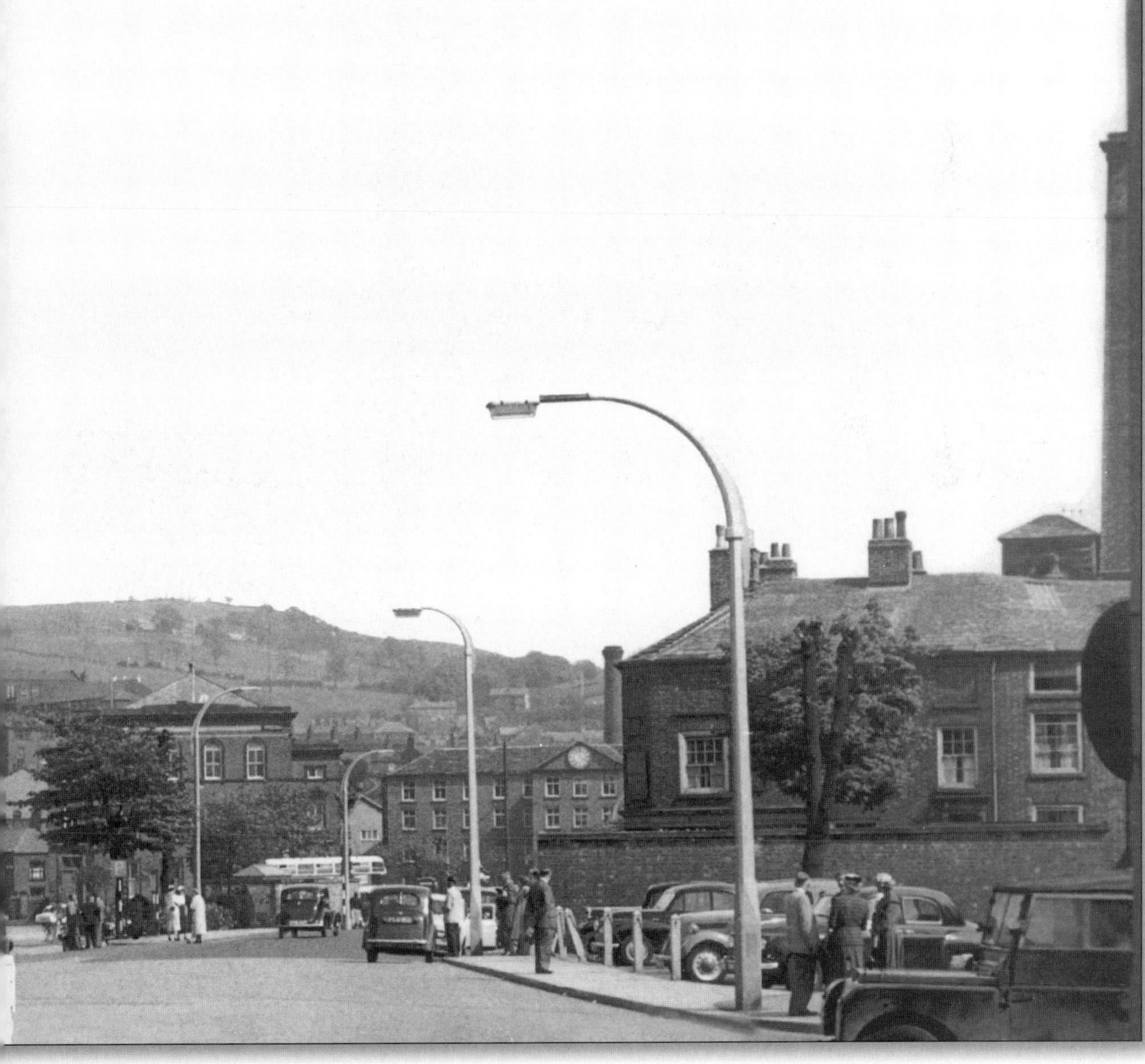

PARK GREEN

CHRISTCHURCH 1903 49462

This view was taken from Catherine Street. For some reason Macclesfield folk pronounce this street name to rhyme with anodyne, or calamine. Somewhere about this point it changes into Bond Street.

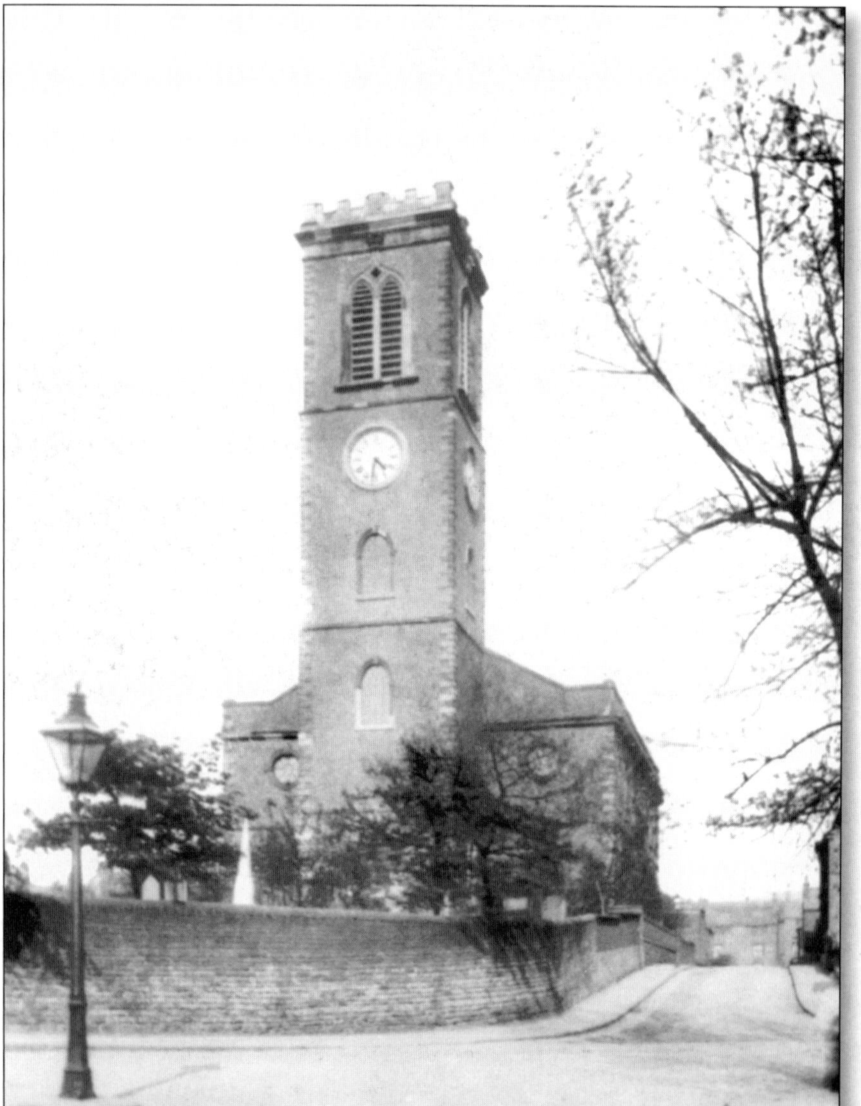

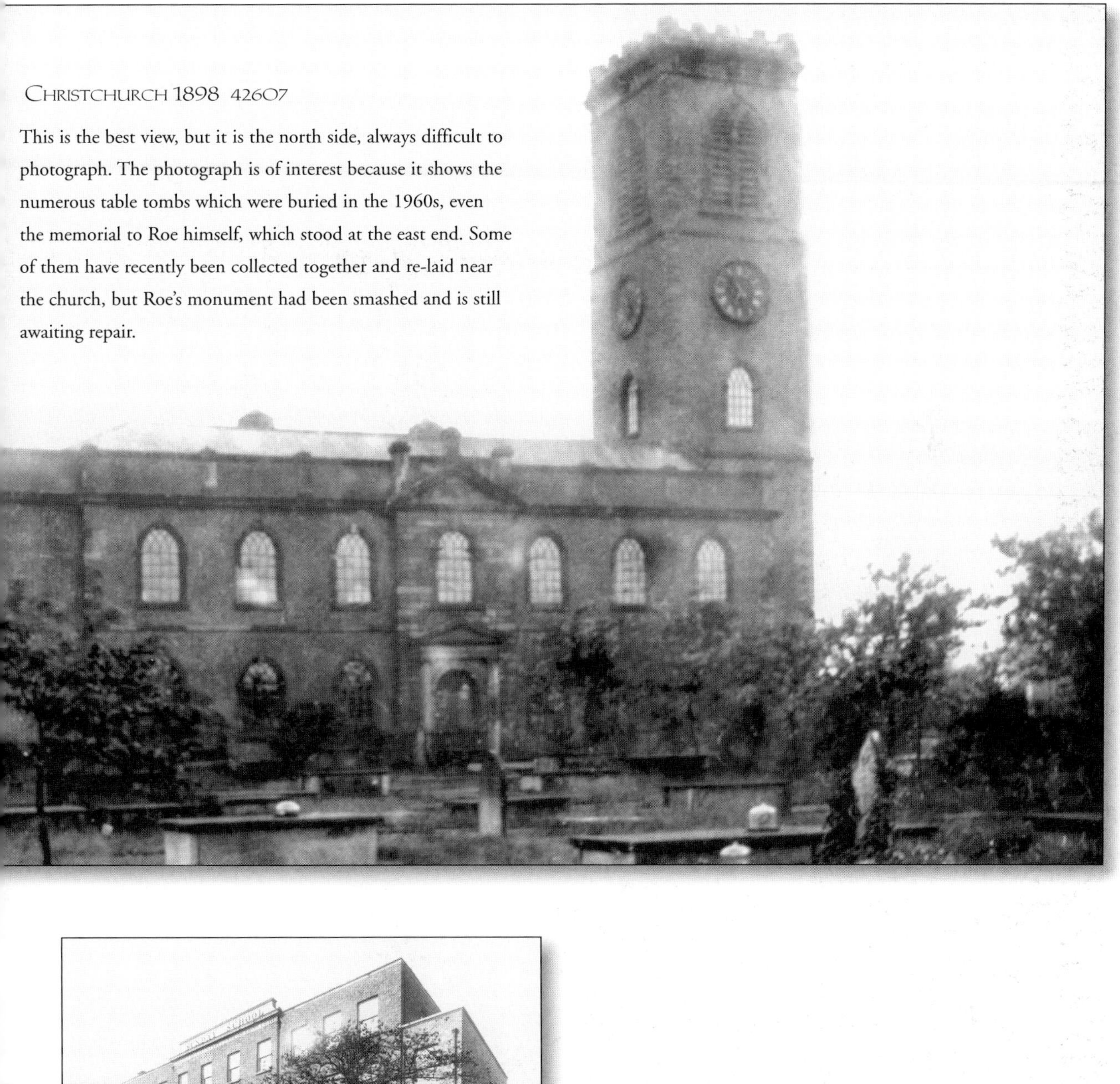

CHRISTCHURCH 1898 42607

This is the best view, but it is the north side, always difficult to photograph. The photograph is of interest because it shows the numerous table tombs which were buried in the 1960s, even the memorial to Roe himself, which stood at the east end. Some of them have recently been collected together and re-laid near the church, but Roe's monument had been smashed and is still awaiting repair.

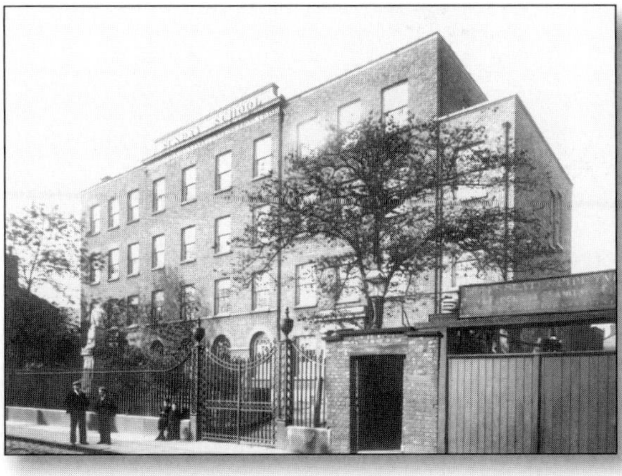

THE SUNDAY SCHOOL 1897 40460

This is now Macclesfield Heritage Centre. The railings all went in the Second World War. The memorial is to John Whitaker, who founded the Sunday School in 1796 'to lessen the sum of human wretchedness'.

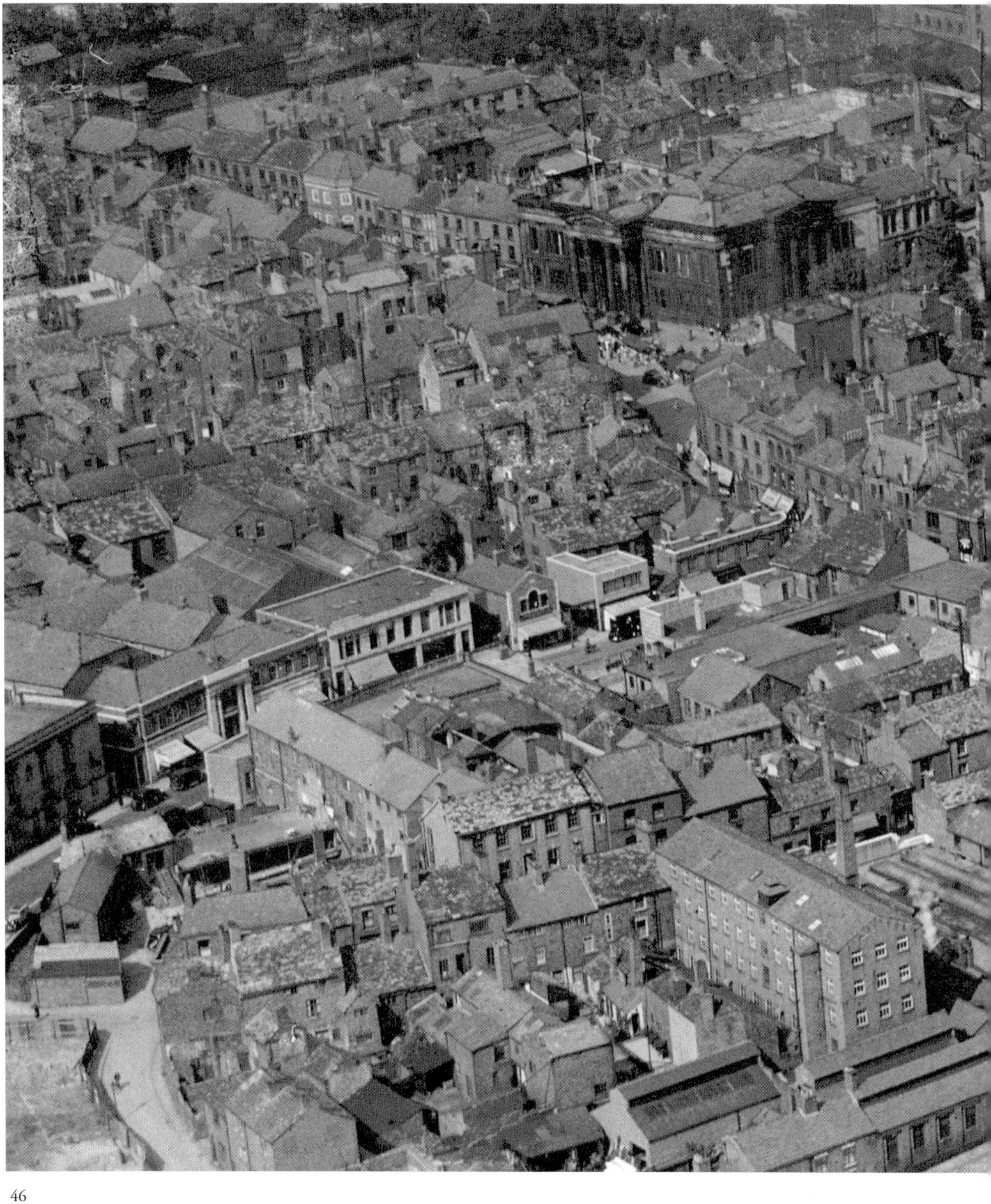

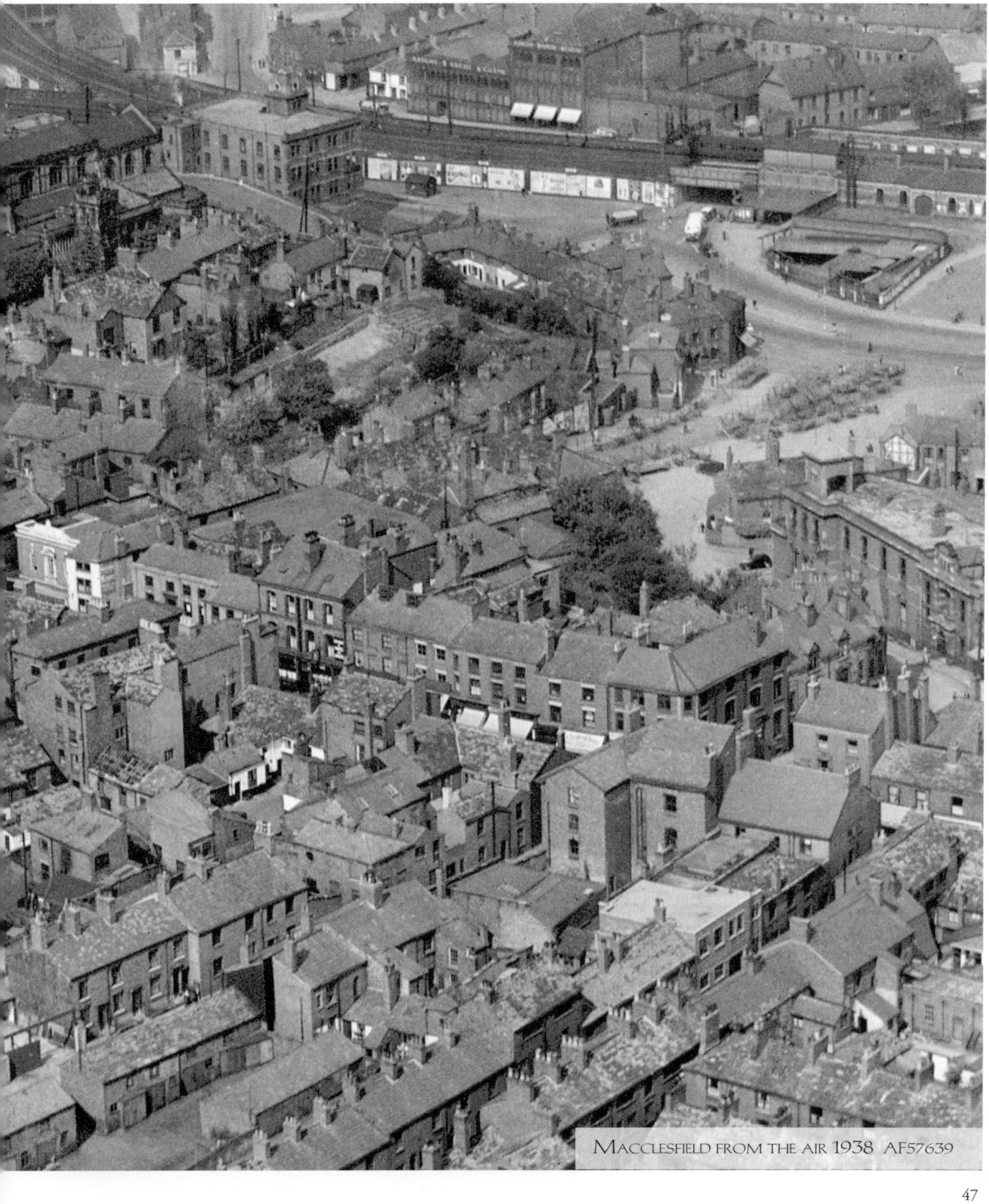

MACCLESFIELD FROM THE AIR 1938 AF57639

GOTHIC

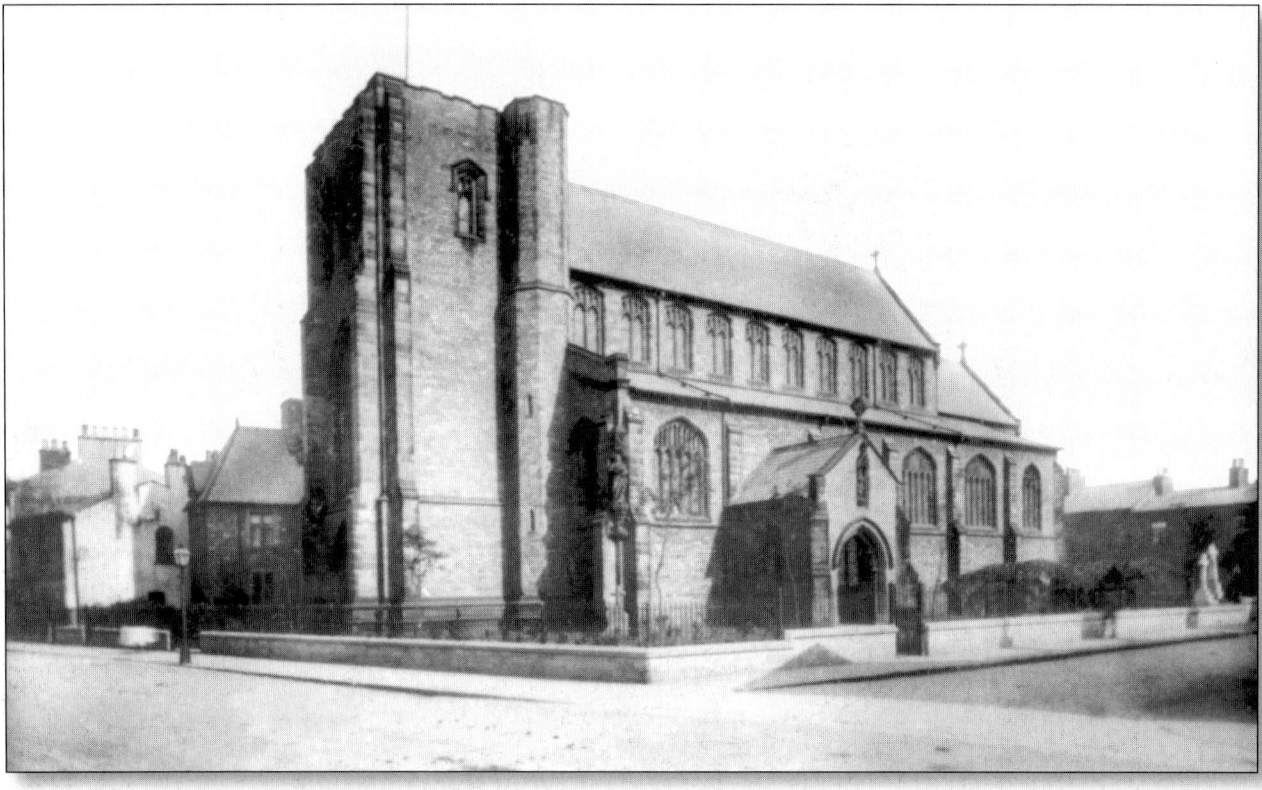

ST ALBAN'S CHURCH 1903 49461

'I have completed the design for the tower but I do not think your funds will enable you to complete it at present', wrote Pugin to Fr Hall in 1838. As we can see, it never has been. The church is also shorter than Pugin intended, and it faces north-south instead of east-west as a church should, because the necessary land was not available.

In the 1840s there was a great turnabout in architectural taste, in fact in the whole of the arts and the crafts. After more than a century of classical taste, sedate, controlled, well-mannered, the world suddenly went Gothic. Everything had to be pointed and spiky. Photographs of the Great Exhibition of 1851 show the incredible profusion of manufactured goods that were on display, many of them in the Gothic taste. The Hereford Screen that was the star of the 1862 Exhibition is a good example. It is brilliantly coloured and moulded, like the Albert Memorial, with lots of gold. Discarded by Hereford Cathedral in the 1960s as a monstrosity of Victoriana, it has recently been superbly restored and is now a star again, this time of the V & A Museum.

This revolution in taste, a turn back to the romance and mystery of the Middle Ages, can be largely laid at the door of a single man. He was Augustus Welby Northmore Pugin, a fanatical convert to Catholicism, and a fanatical convert to Gothic. He it was who gave Barry's Houses of Parliament their gorgeous Gothic dress, inside and out. As it happens, Pugin built a church, St Alban's, in Macclesfield (49461, above). Although it must be admitted that it is a church of no great beauty, it is our only building by a truly famous architect. It was largely paid for by the Earl of Shrewsbury, with whom Pugin, an outspoken character with no social graces, had formed an unlikely friendship. Their common ground was the revival of Catholic faith and church building. Shrewsbury and Pugin achieved astonishing feats of building, especially in Staffordshire and the Midlands, so

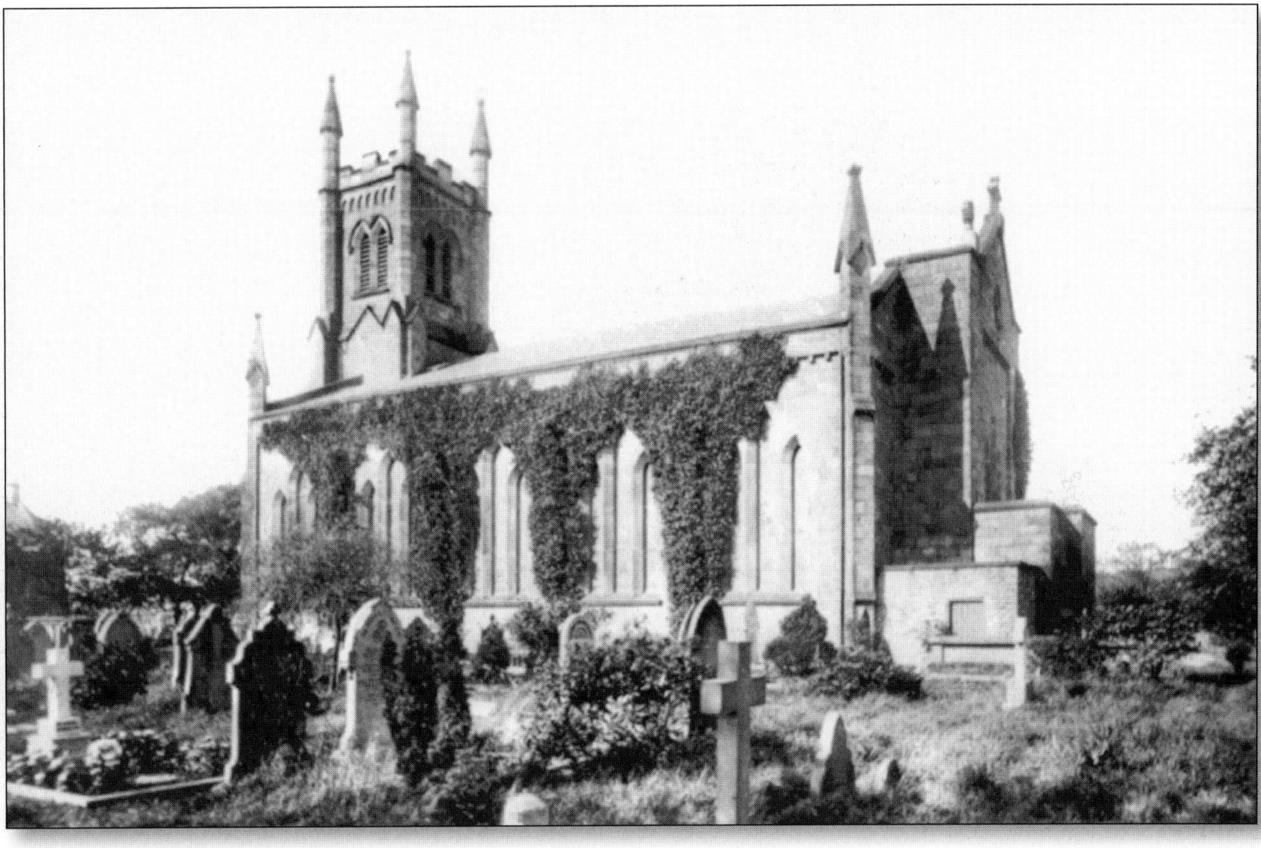

HURDSFIELD CHURCH 1897 40457

The triple windows are a simple reference to the church's dedication, Holy Trinity.

much so that the noble but overspent Earl was forced to close his vast mansion, Alton Towers, and live abroad, and Pugin worked himself to an early death.

Other architects followed more slowly. There are a whole string of churches by William Hayley of Manchester in the area, and it can be seen that through the series he was gradually learning how to build Gothic. The first was St John's, Bollington, 1834, little more than a classical box with Gothic dress. Among the many speeches that accompanied the cold collation in honour of its consecration was a proposal to launch an appeal for another new church.

Such was the heady pace of church building in those days that the next one, Holy Trinity, Hurdsfield (40457, above), opened in 1837. Soon it was followed by St James', Sutton (49459, pages 52-53), in 1840, and then St Paul's on Brook Street (40456, page 54) in 1844; all were by Hayley. Each one shows an advance in Gothic expertise; by the time he got to St Paul's, Hayley was able to design a full-blown Gothic church with elegant Gothic arcades within and a fine steeple outside, still one of the landmarks of the town.

All these churches were certainly needed. Macclesfield had grown phenomenally in the early 19th century, and social provision, education and the basic necessities of life were all lacking. The churches were the first agents of change for the better. The heroic efforts of Henry Briant, the first vicar of St Paul's, are a good example. Distressed by the hordes of street children roaming his parish, he collected 100 or so in a dilapidated building opposite the church; here they could be fed, sheltered, taught to read and write,

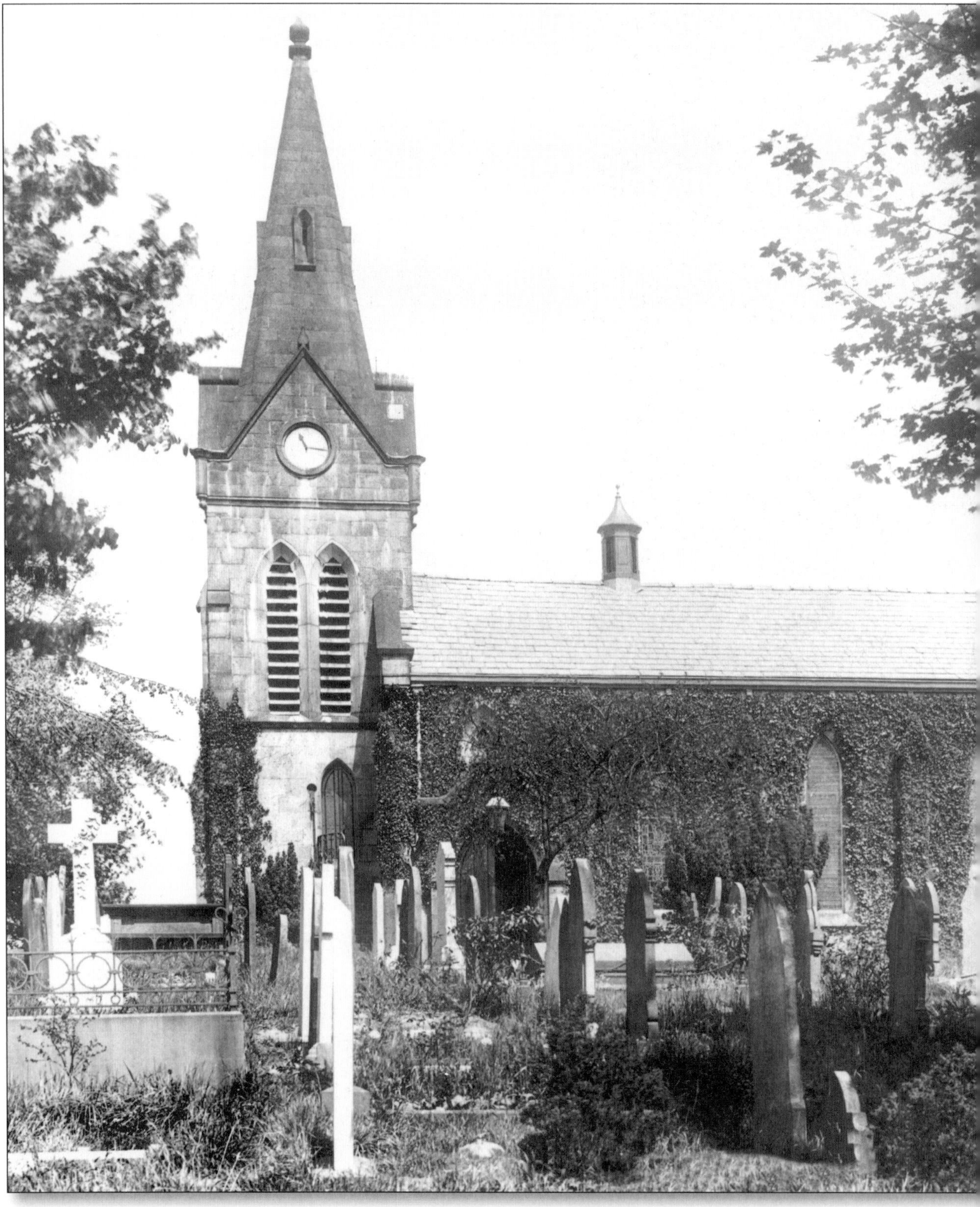

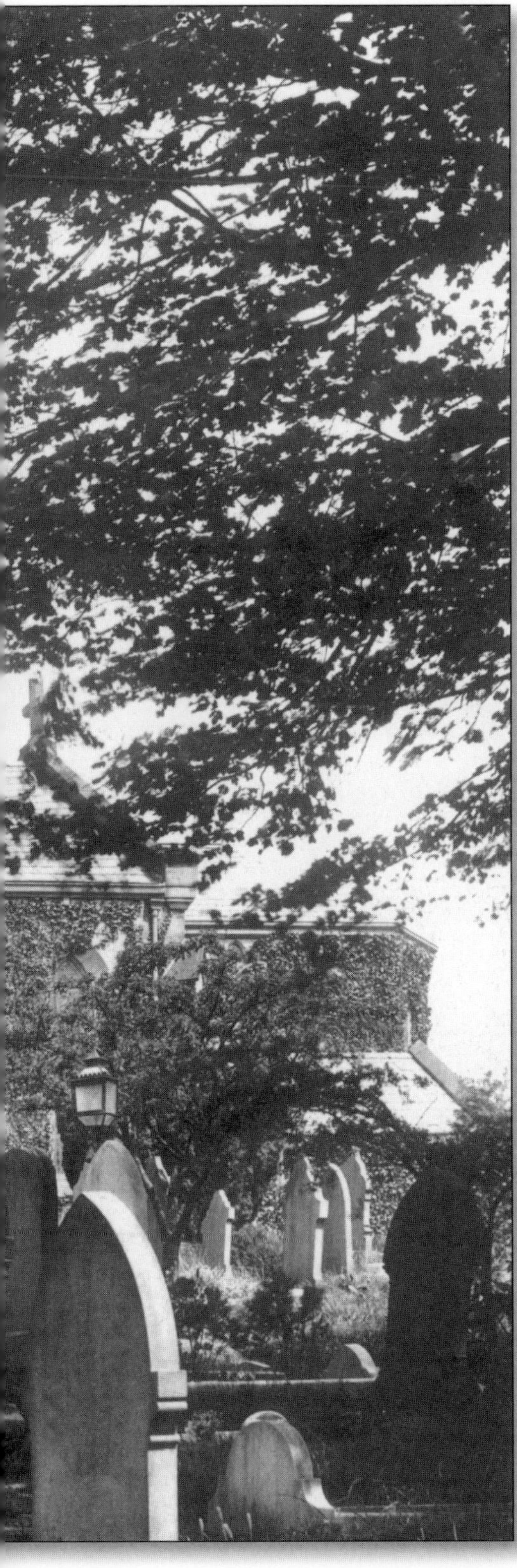

and in due course given the skills to earn their living. Eventually in 1866 a new building called the Industrial School, or more popularly the Ragged School, was constructed. It still stands on Brook Street; its size is an astonishing testimony to the size of the problem. Lord Shaftesbury said he would far rather be President of the Ragged Schools than President of the Royal Academy.

Raising money for a new church was difficult. Macclesfield was not rich, so there were no wealthy patrons on hand. A church like St Paul's would have cost about £4000. Present-day churchwardens might scoff at such an amount, but it was a huge sum to raise then. One way that the money could be raised was by producing a lithograph of the intended church, often in somewhat idealised surroundings, and then selling copies of the prints - see the illustration. Most of the mid-Victorian churches in town seem to have done this; a framed example can often be found hanging in the vestry.

Dissenting chapels were in their early days deliberately unobtrusive, even hidden away down semi-secret ginnels and passageways. King Edward Street Chapel in Macclesfield, built in 1689, is just like this; it is almost entirely invisible, although very charming inside. This is because their place in society was uncertain, and they were occasionally subject to mob violence. Slowly they became more confident and came out into the open. They were still usually distinct from established churches in their architecture, and never had towers. A proud example is the Methodist New Connection Chapel of 1836, now Harvest Printers, on Park Lane. Only in the 1850s did the fashion for Gothic start to affect the non-conformist churches, and even then it was uncommon to build a tower. 'Sheer vanity' seems to have been the general opinion of such excesses.

ST JAMES'S CHURCH 1903 49459

This is not a beautiful design in itself, but just right for its beautiful situation on a knoll surrounded by bigger hills, and very successful as a village church. The two big pepperpots on the roof were ventilators.

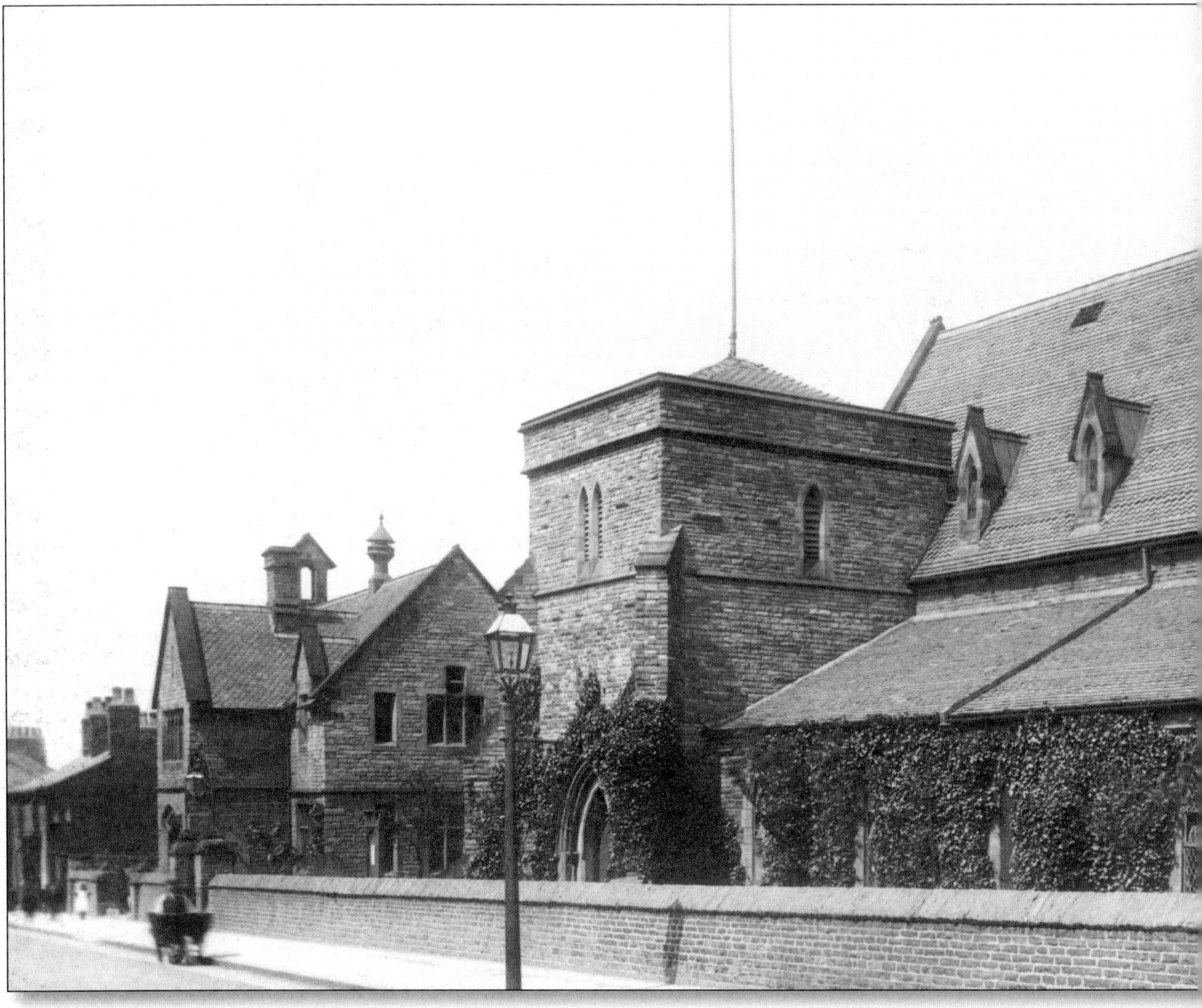

ST PETER'S CHURCH 1903 49460

Like St Alban's five years earlier, St Peter's opened in 1849 without the top of its tower. It was designed by a Staffordshire builder and architect (and amateur strongman!), James Trubshaw. But unlike St Alban's, the tower was finally completed in 1910. The eight melodious bells were hung in 1947 as a war memorial. Beyond the church we can see the pretty school, which unfortunately closed in 1984.

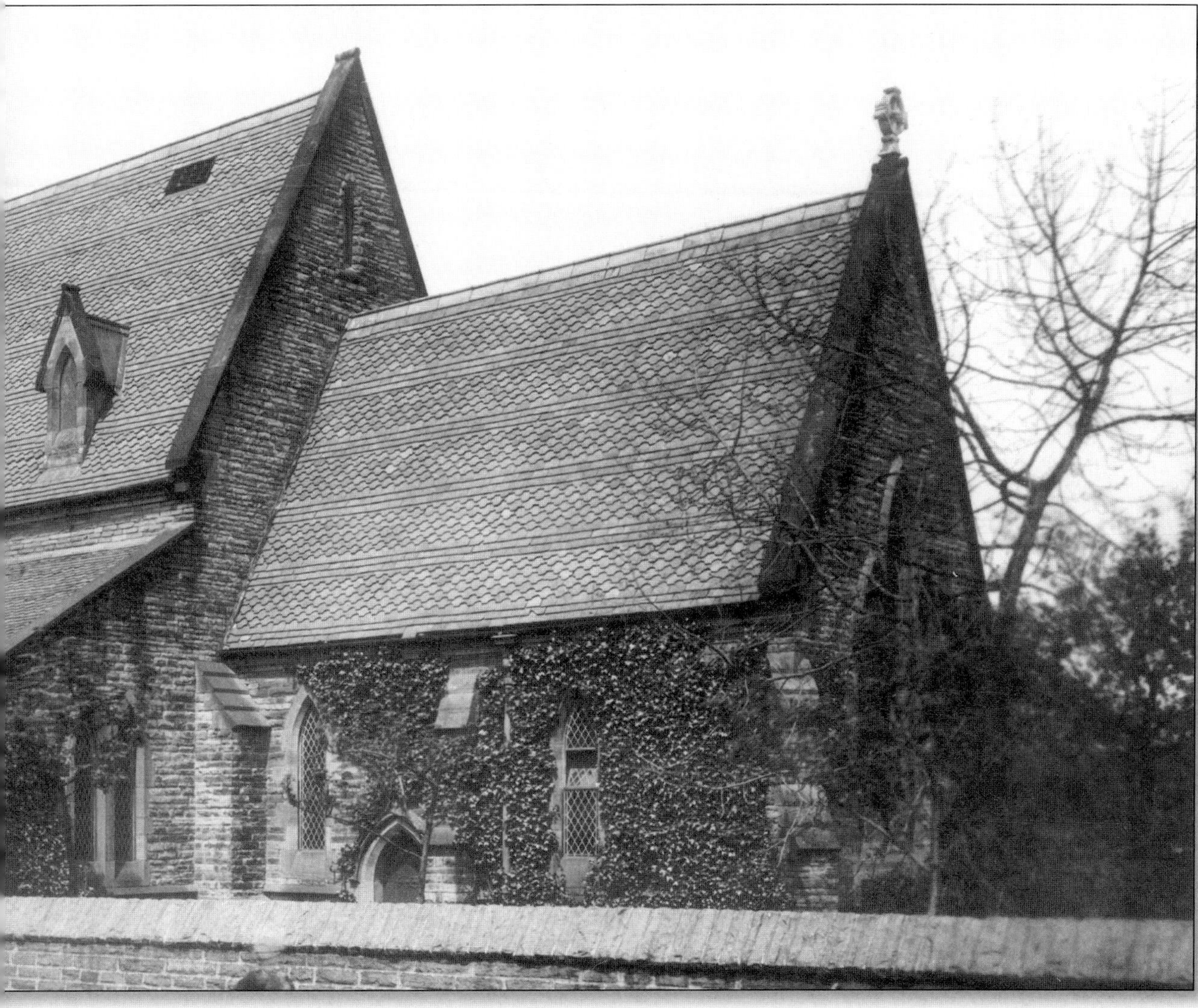

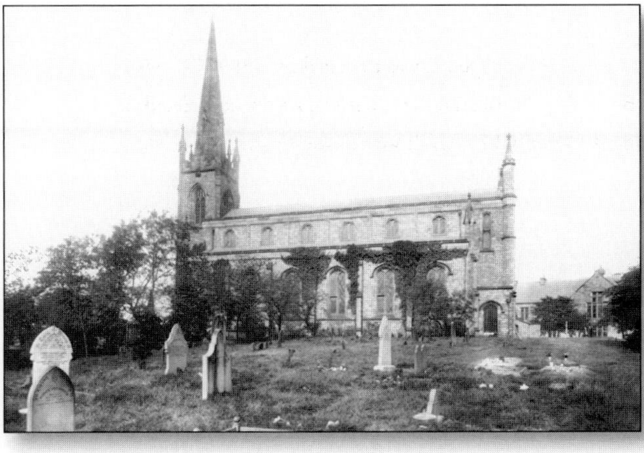

ST PAUL'S CHURCH 1897 40456

It is recorded that the first vicar, the Rev Henry Briant, climbed to the top of the spire in 1844 when the topmost stone was put in place, a feat imitated by the author when the spire had to be repaired in 1979. The church has been thrown into even greater prominance by the building of the 'by-pass' which cuts through the middle of the town.

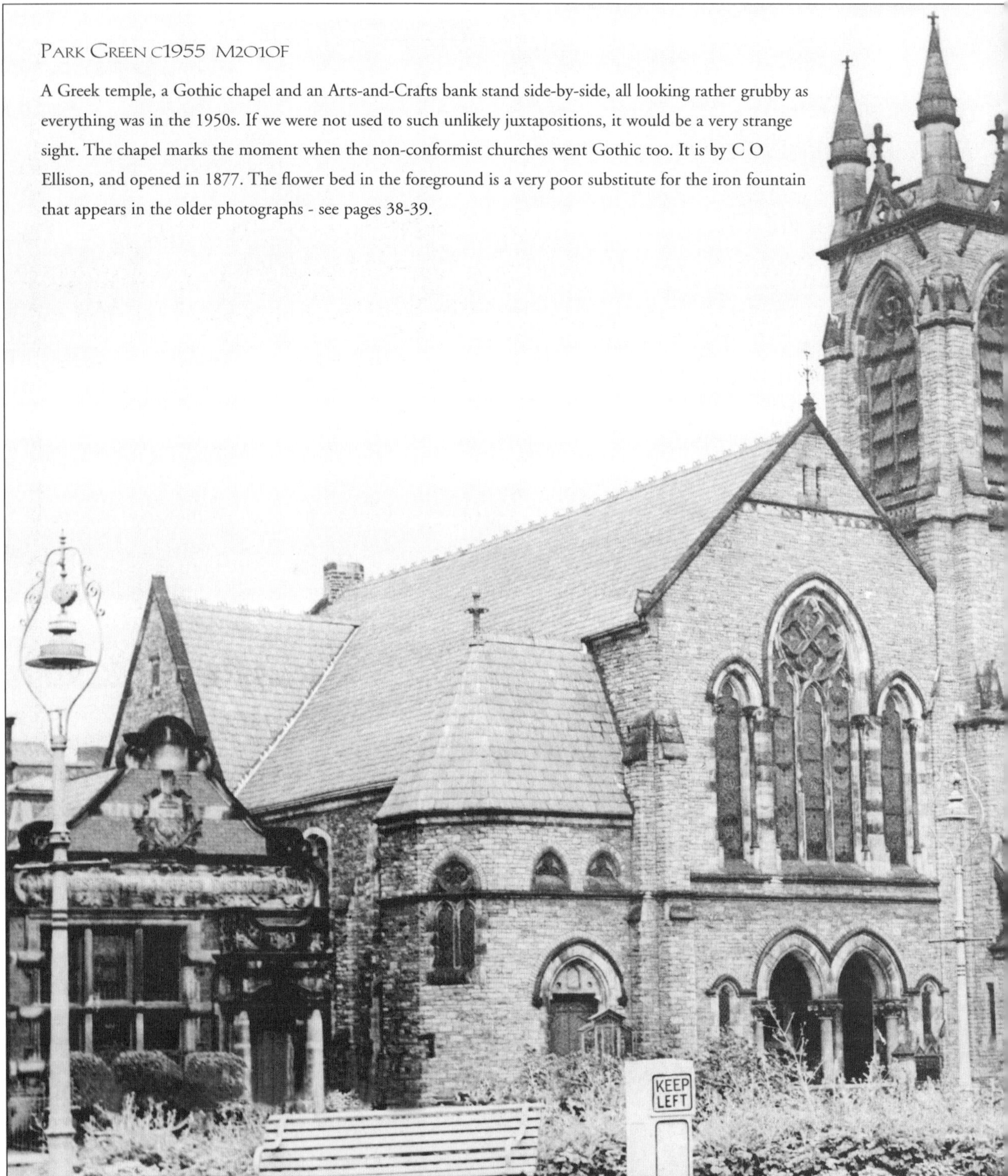

PARK GREEN c1955 M201OF

A Greek temple, a Gothic chapel and an Arts-and-Crafts bank stand side-by-side, all looking rather grubby as everything was in the 1950s. If we were not used to such unlikely juxtapositions, it would be a very strange sight. The chapel marks the moment when the non-conformist churches went Gothic too. It is by C O Ellison, and opened in 1877. The flower bed in the foreground is a very poor substitute for the iron fountain that appears in the older photographs - see pages 38-39.

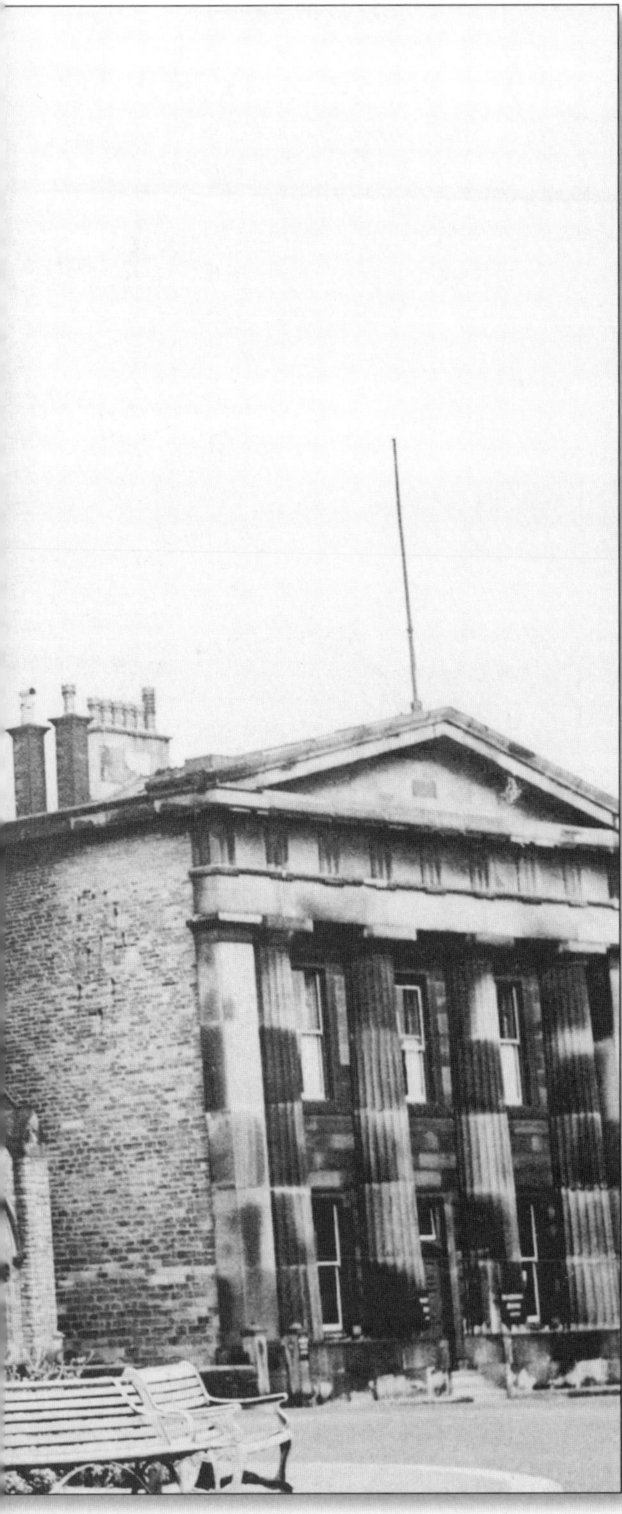

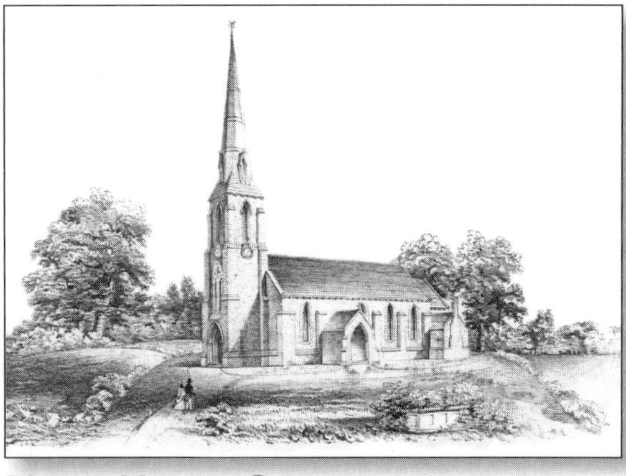

VIEW OF HENBURY CHURCH

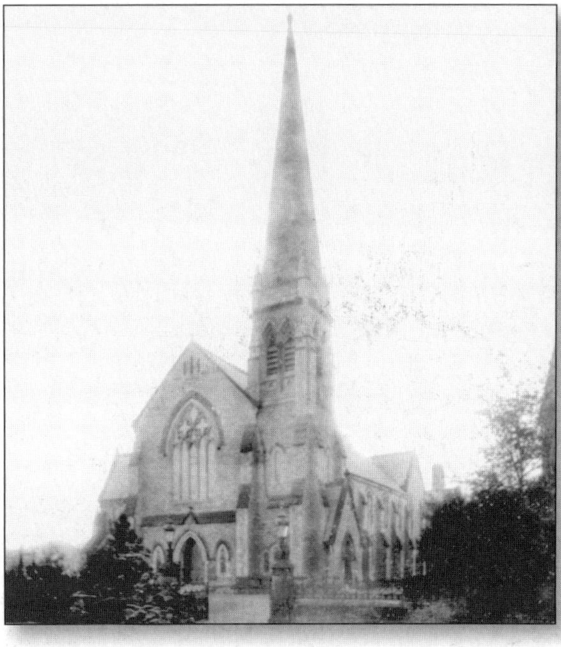

WESLEYAN TRINITY CHAPEL 1897 40450

This chapel was opened in 1874. With its soaring spire and Gothic façade, it looks as though it could also be by C O Ellison (see M2010F, left). Ellison also designed a Methodist church at Frodsham with a spire, called Trinity Chapel. Today a neat development of old people's flats stands here; there is little evidence of the past except the stone front wall and the name: Trinity.

BRABNER'S MAP

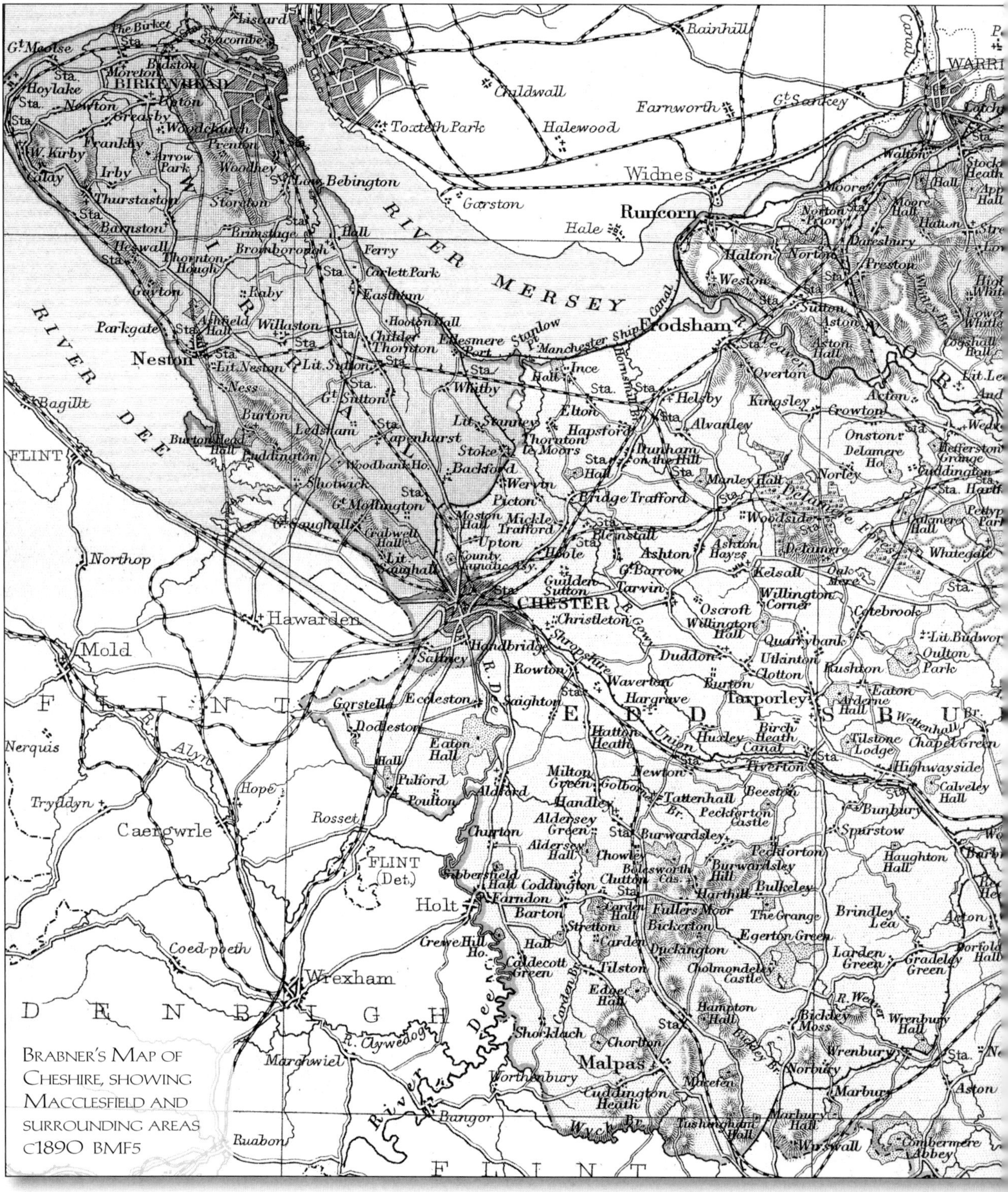

BRABNER'S MAP OF CHESHIRE, SHOWING MACCLESFIELD AND SURROUNDING AREAS c1890 BMF5

Brabner's Map

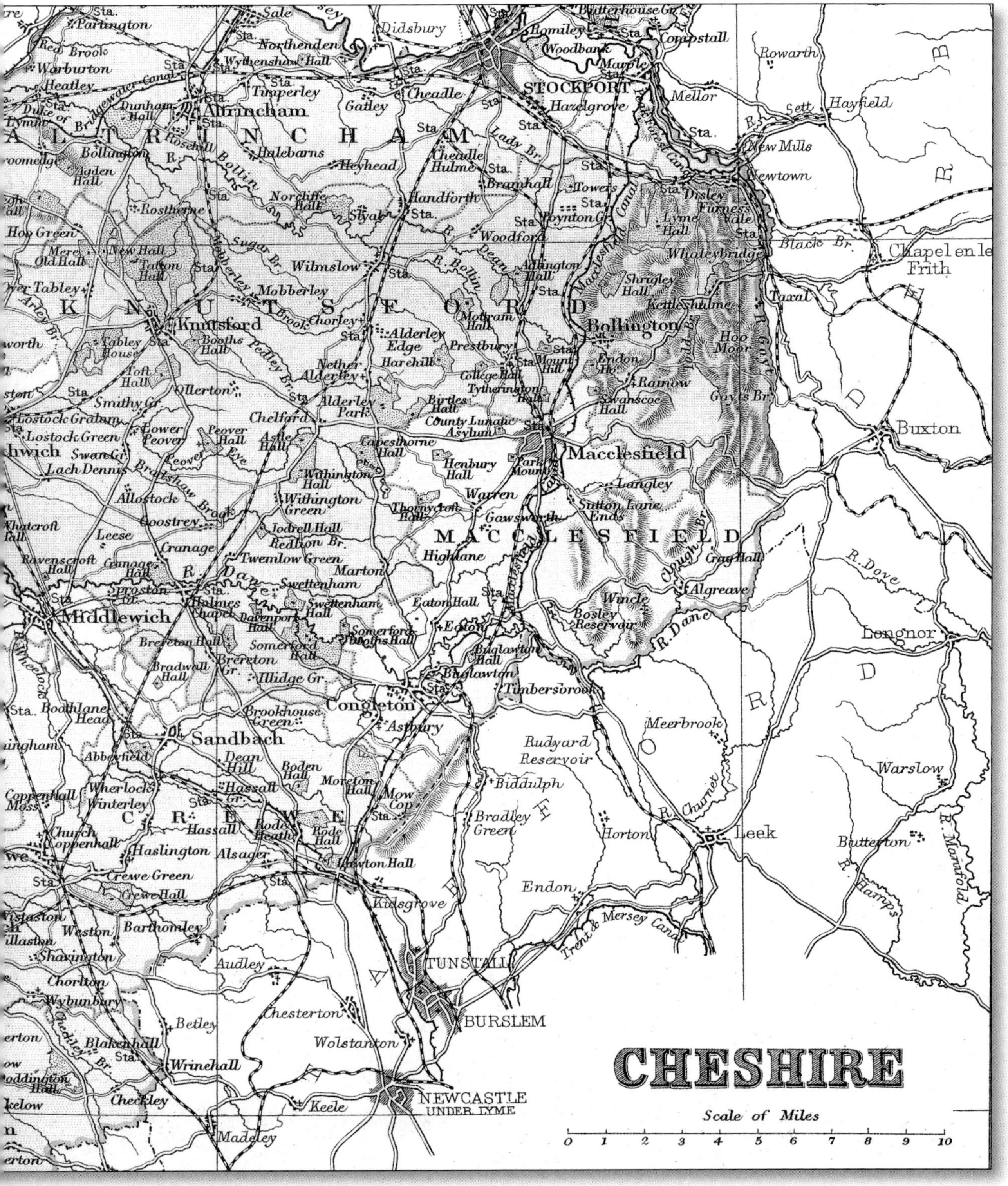

THE TOWN HALL 1897 40440

James Stevens usually liked to build in a Gothic style, but here noblesse oblige. He could hardly extend Goodwin's severely classical Town Hall in anything other than more of the same. The join between the two is quite clearly visible in this picture; Goodwin's building is on the right, Stevens's new front is on the left.

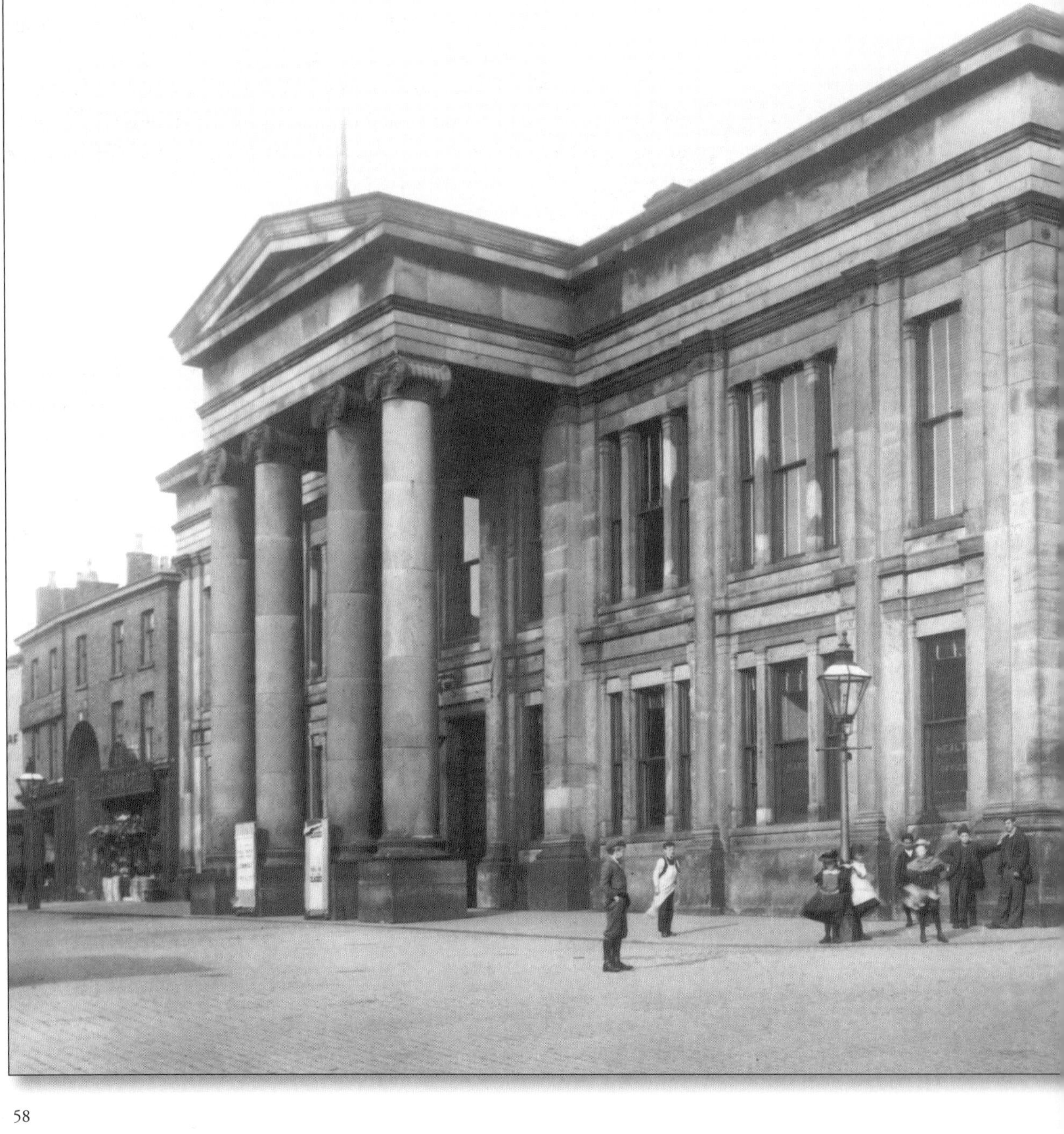

THE WEST END, PUBLIC WORKS AND JAMES STEVENS

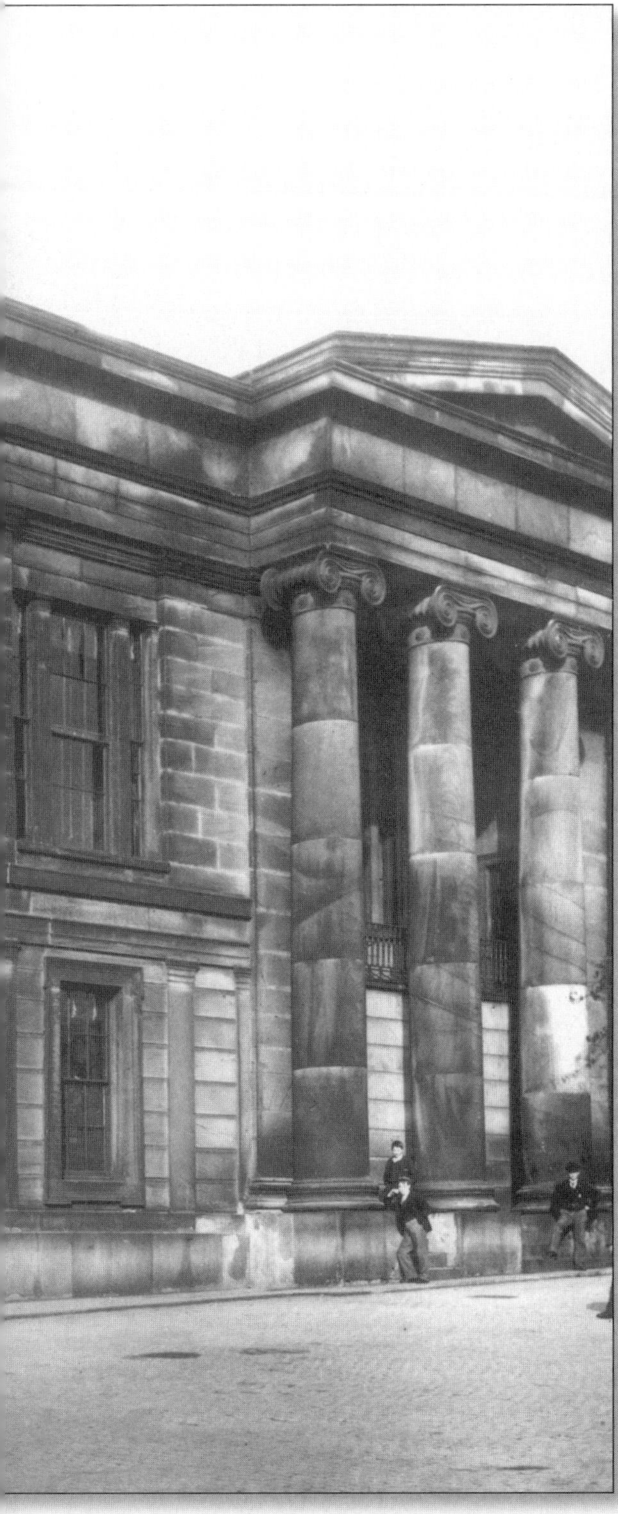

Macclesfield by 1850 was an overcrowded, filthy, lively, inventive mill town. It was the centre of the silk trade, full of little terraced cottages and clacking mills. It had grown so fast that social care, medical care, schools and even space to be buried in had fallen far behind the need.

After 1850 there was something of a slump in the silk trade and the growth rate slowed down considerably, so Macclesfield never became another Manchester. This was when Macclesfield caught up with itself. It was the age of public building and social improvement, when churches, technical and art schools, hospitals, parks, the museum and the cemetery all came into being.

One architect is particularly associated with this phase in the town's development, being involved in nearly all the schemes to improve the lot of the townsfolk. He was James Stevens. So many of James Stevens' buildings appear on these pages that one wonders whether he was consulted by Mr Frith.

Stevens died aged 76 in 1902, so that means he was born in 1826. He was not Macclesfield born and bred, but he adopted the town and the town adopted him. He was actually born in London and educated at Prescot in Lancashire, and then articled as a young architect in Liverpool. He came here as a young man for the Baths competition in 1849, and made Macclesfield his home, settling at 173 Chester Road. The baths are no longer with us, and nor is Davenport Street that they stood on. It is said that the dirty water from the baths was used to fill the tanks of the railway engines below! The Barracks (49470, pages 62-63) on Crompton Road came next in 1858-59, in conjunction with Mr Pownall of London.

Soon after the Barracks came the Town Hall Extension of 1869-71. Stevens was commissioned to extend the original building. His extension is what we usually think of as the front, facing Chestergate (40440, left). The side facing over the churchyard is the original building. Inside is a fine iron-balustraded staircase leading up to the new council chamber. On the stairs is a statue of Artemis by Hamo Thorneycroft, one of the most famous sculptors of the Victorian age. Macclesfield has produced a number of fine sculptors; Thorneycroft was related to the Hollands of Broken Cross. The Town Hall is spoiled today by an unsuccessful cleaning operation which has left it looking blotchy, which is a pity. The flat roof of the portico is excellent for fireworks.

THE WEST END, PUBLIC WORKS AND JAMES STEVENS

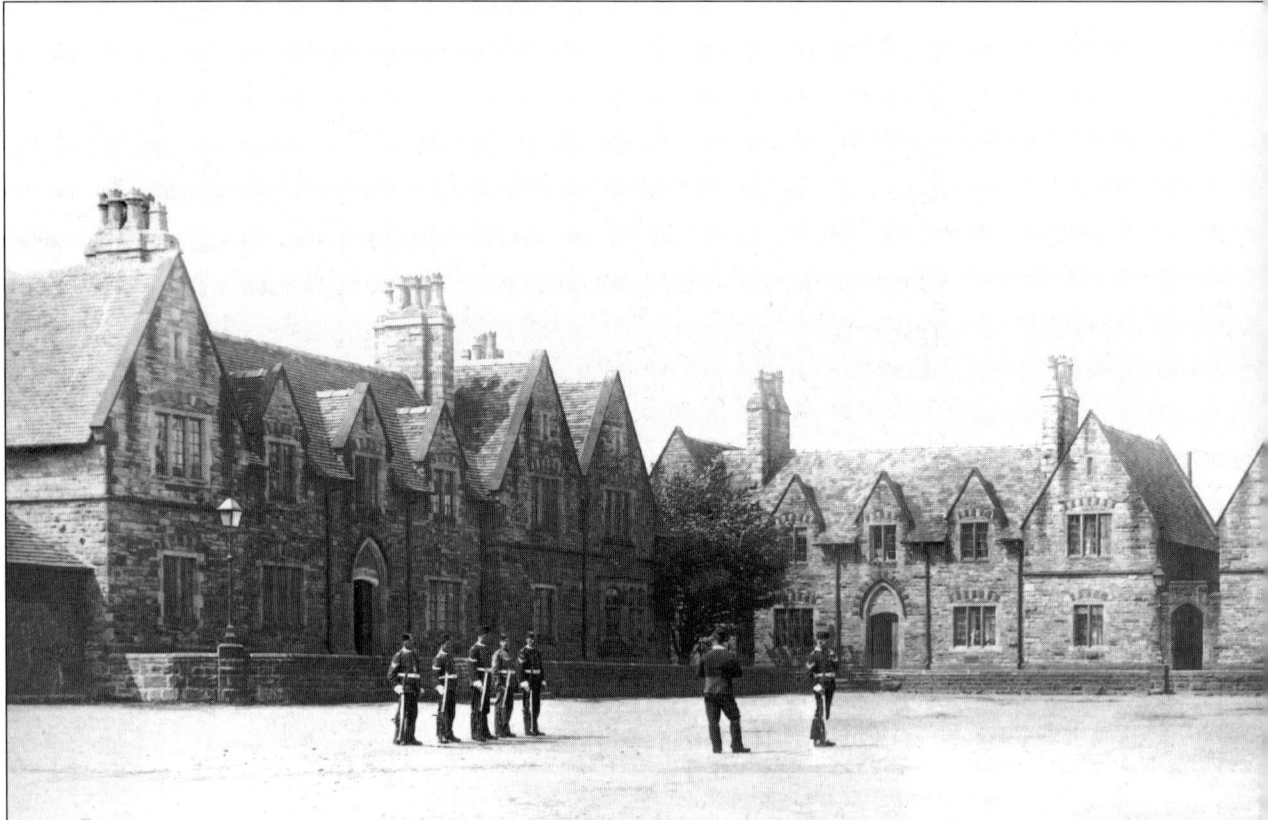

THE BARRACKS 1903 49470

Toy soldiers parade in a toy castle! No doubt it seemed serious at the time. Amazingly, this scene has changed scarcely at all in a hundred years. The dusty parade ground is still there, although now we are more likely to be mown down by children on trikes than by marching soldiers. Some new houses have been built on the Crompton Road front, but the barrack blocks at the back, seen here, are unchanged.

The Chadwick Free Library of 1876 on Park Green (40451, page 64), incorporating a reading room, lending department, and reference section, was one of Stevens's finest works. There had been other libraries in the town, including that of the Useful Knowledge Society housed next door, but this was the first to be free and open to all. Literacy and the dissemination of knowledge was important to the developing town.

At much the same time that Macclesfield began its social improvement, a penniless but upwardly mobile youth called Andrew Carnegie, a recent immigrant from Scotland to America, obtained his first taste of knowledge from a library in Pittsburg. He never forgot the lesson, and in due course became the greatest donor of libraries the world is ever likely to see. Carnegie, who became the richest man on earth through shrewd investment, thought that his investment in public libraries was the most worthwhile thing he had ever done. No doubt Chadwick, with justification, could have thought so too.

Park Green Library served the town for more than a century. Today the library is more spaciously housed in what is almost certainly another Stevens building, the Manchester and Liverpool Bank of 1881 on the Market Place, which has been judiciously extended by the County.

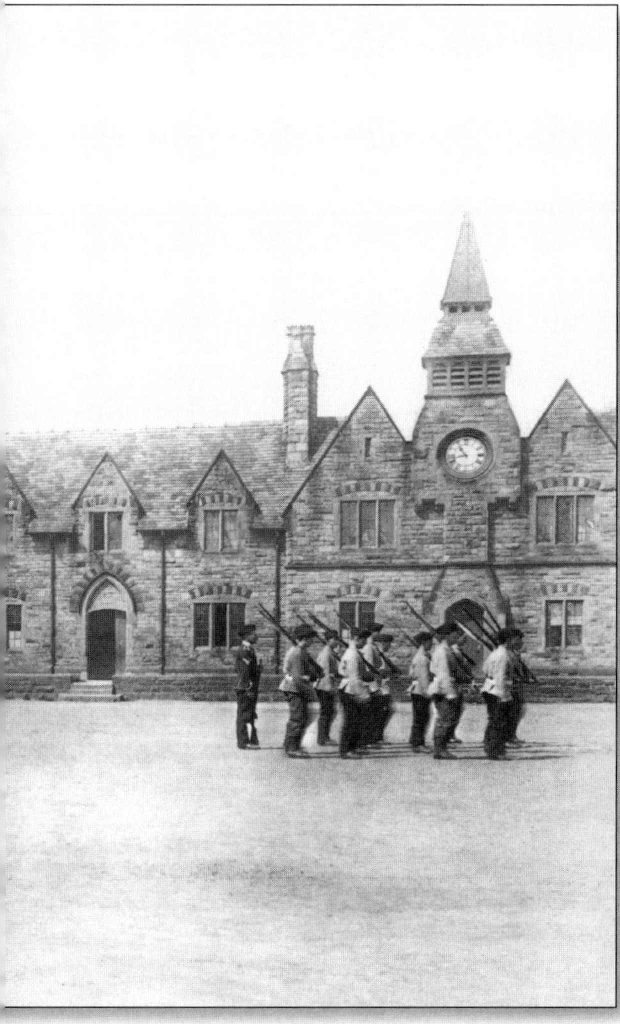

The School of Art (40451, page 64) was built in 1879 next to the library on Park Street. Its purpose was to train up designers for the silk industry. Its most famous pupil was probably Charles Tunnicliffe, a naturally gifted farmer's son from Sutton who became a wonderful artist of wildlife and a prolific illustrator of books. The Technical School was built on the other side of the library in 1898. Stevens designed the Technical School in Crewe too.

In 1882 he started a complete restoration of the Parish Church with enlargements of the chancel and north aisle and new vestries. The project ran into difficulties because of all the burials inside the church that were endangering the foundations, and it also ran out of money. Sir Arthur Blomfield finished the job, and got all the credit. The chancel, with its terrazzo floor and mosaic of St Michael, is Stevens's.

Macclesfield Infirmary (40443 and 40444, page 65) was the greatest boon to the town and Stevens's biggest work. It originated in a bequest by Joseph Tunnicliffe, who left £35,000 in 1859. Thomas Swanwick MD added £1,500 as an endowment, which was matched by Mr William Barnett's £2,000 in 1871. The rest of the cost was met by Macclesfield people digging in their own pockets; hence the outrage when it was sold.

Most of Stevens's work is Gothic, but the Town Hall is as classical as can be, and the Infirmary is a French chateau. Victorian architects were nothing if not versatile. The Infirmary was built all in stone: buff ashlar contrasted with pink Teggsnose rubble, just like the author's house. The hugely extravagant and impractical front steps were removed in 1978 to make a new gynaecology ward. 'Sheer Vandalism', thundered the local paper. Worse was to follow: the Infirmary was closed down and demolished altogether, and the site was sold off for a supermarket. The pink stone was used again for Sainsbury's store, together with some carved coats of arms, but otherwise the Infirmary is no more.

Although surrounded by fine countryside, Macclesfield folk would not have had the time or the means to get out of the town easily, so the parks were needed. The first park in the country to be provided at public expense was Birkenhead Park, which was completed in 1846. It was designed by William Paxton, the famous head gardener of Chatsworth, who was later to be knighted for his design of the Crystal Palace.

West Park (M2014, page 66-67) is not much later in date. It was our first public park, and is still the most popular. The designer here was William Barron. He was head gardener to the Earl and Countess of Harrington at the fantastic Elvaston Castle in Derbyshire. He was allowed by the Earl to come and lay out Macclesfield's West Park in 1851.

William Barron was one of the heroic and celebrated Victorian gardeners, like Paxton. He was a specialist in moving full-grown trees, and excelled in topiary and rockwork. The garden at Elvaston Castle (see illustration, page 66) was very famous, but it was never seen by the public. Its fame came from the gardening magazines, through which

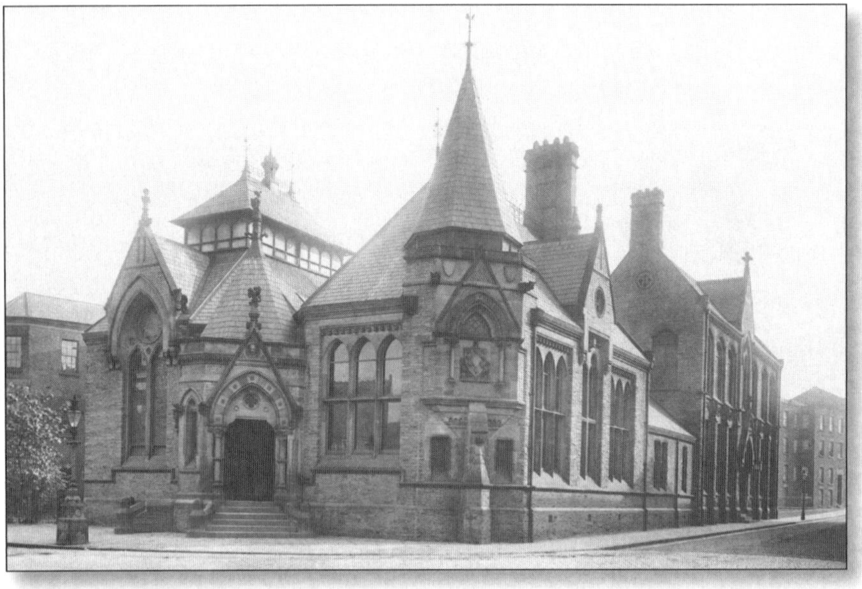

ABOVE: THE FREE LIBRARY 1897 40451

This fine photograph shows the Chadwick Library, opened in 1876, and the School of Art of 1879 to its right, but not, it will be noticed, the Technical School on the left, which was built just a year after this picture (compare with 49466 on page 38).

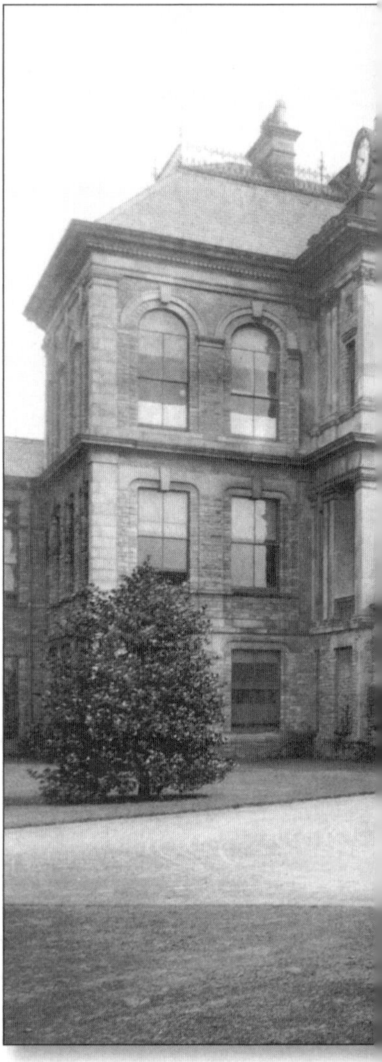

Barron was one of the star presenters of the day. The garden's extreme privacy came about because the Earl and Countess had been ostracised by society, and the Earl decided to get his own back by making a wonderful garden and then not letting anyone see it. The garden was also a homage to his beautiful young bride, Maria Foote; but she was unwittingly the cause of the trouble. She was an actress, and was thus considered a totally unsuitable match for a nobleman. Such was the hypocrisy of the age that it was perfectly acceptable to take a young actress as a mistress, but totally unacceptable to marry her.

By the gate of the park is the West Park Museum. This was built by a remarkable lady, Miss Marianne Brocklehurst, to house her Egyptian collection plus other curios such as the panda, which has been such a favourite of Macclesfield children for so long. The Egyptian items were collected by her in 1873-74 during a Nile cruise on a sailing boat; she recorded her adventures in a hand-written notebook illustrated by her own lively water-colours. They paint a marvellous picture of a surprisingly unpriggish Victorian lady in a land that filled her with wonder. The panda has recently been conserved. For years it was rather dingy and faded, but now it is smartly black-and-white again. By the 1860s, Macclesfield's churchyards were all well and truly full up; the old church's was so full that it prejudiced not only the safety of the building but the health of the neighbours. Not without some difficulty, the Corporation duly acquired a fine site for a cemetery (42602, page 75). It was continuous with West Park, but divided from it by a valley and a brook. Roadmaking, landscaping and the building of three chapels took the total cost to nearly £12,000. It is a pity that the Frith photographers did not photograph the cemetery chapels; they are architecturally outrageous, particularly the one which is now converted to a studio. Victorian architects seem to have lost all their

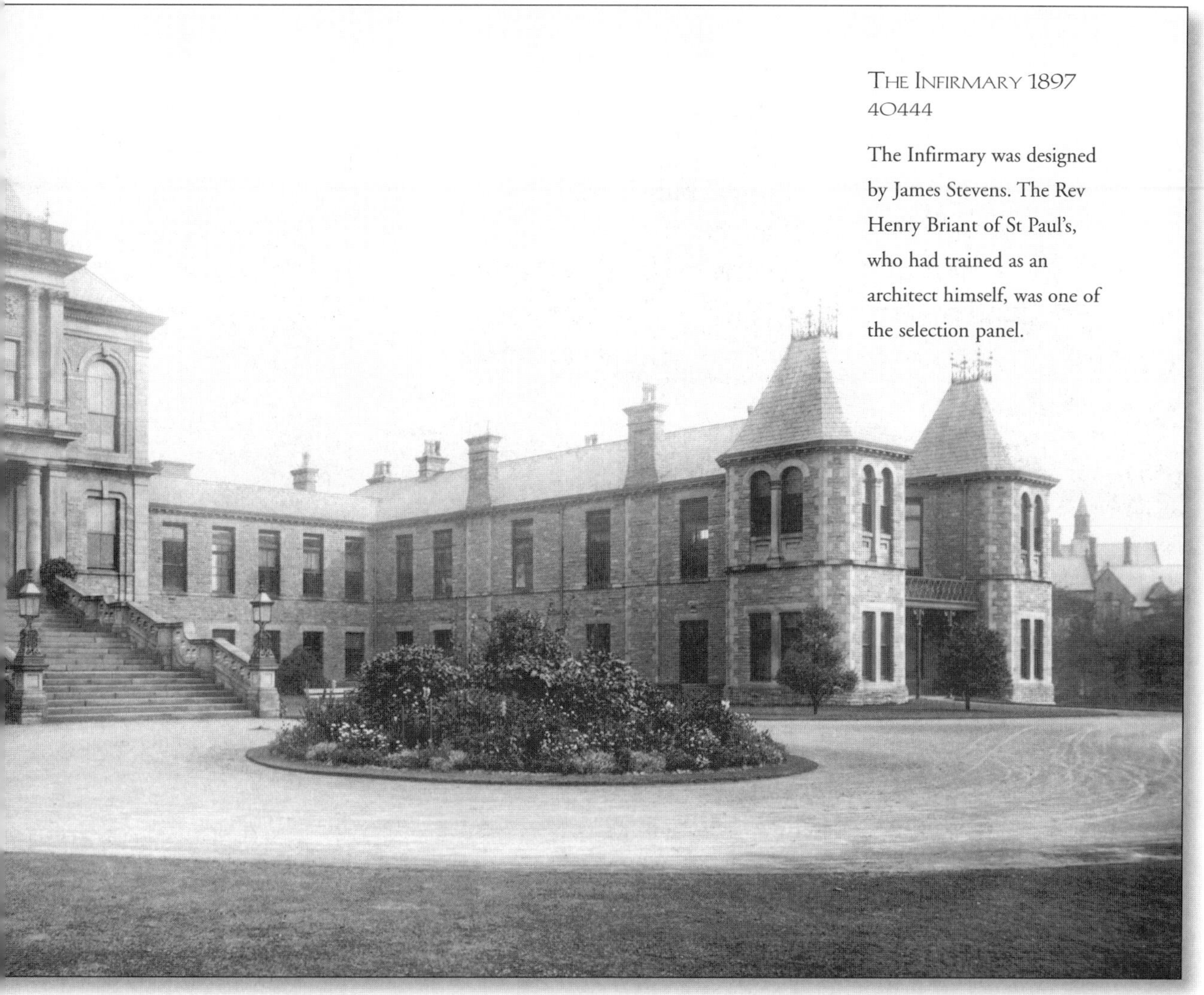

THE INFIRMARY 1897
40444

The Infirmary was designed by James Stevens. The Rev Henry Briant of St Paul's, who had trained as an architect himself, was one of the selection panel.

THE INFIRMARY 1897
40443

The Infirmary opened on 2 October 1872 for 60 in-patients, with quarters for nurses and a training school. It was designed on the pavilion system, like Parkside Asylum, but was less extended.

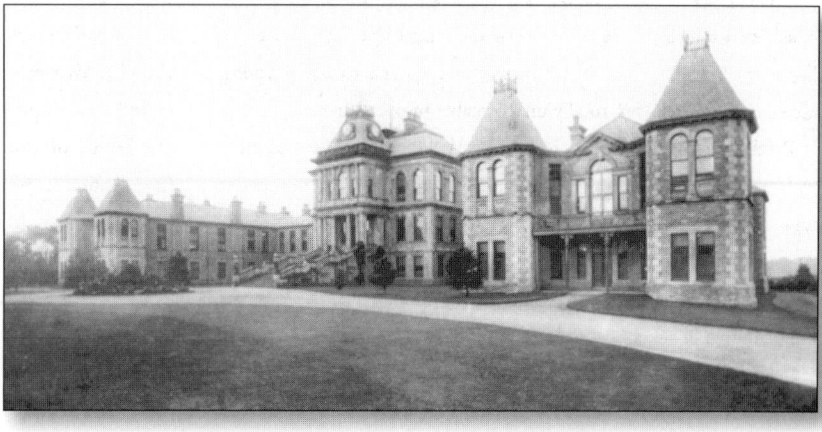

inhibitions when dealing with death.

The cemetery was declared open on 17 May 1866; the event was not accompanied by the customary junketing, such as that described previously for the opening of Victoria Park. Evidently it was felt that in this case, a quiet restraint was the proper thing.

Mental illness was a major industry in the 19th century. Each county had its own asylum. They were monumental establishments, usually excellently built and run and often set in extensive grounds. It is difficult to say why they were needed in such quantity; it is perhaps easier to understand how the coming of drug treatments in the 1950s and social and political changes in the 1970s made such huge institutions redundant.

Parkside Hospital, the County Asylum for Cheshire (40454, page 74), was built in exactly the same year as the Infirmary, although it opened first, on 8 May 1871. The architect was Robert Griffiths of Stafford. He made a speciality of this new building type, just as Gilbert Scott had made a speciality of workhouses, such as the one which became West Park Hospital, before he became famous. Parkside is a huge complex designed in a grand symmetry that is more apparent on an aerial photograph than on the ground (rather

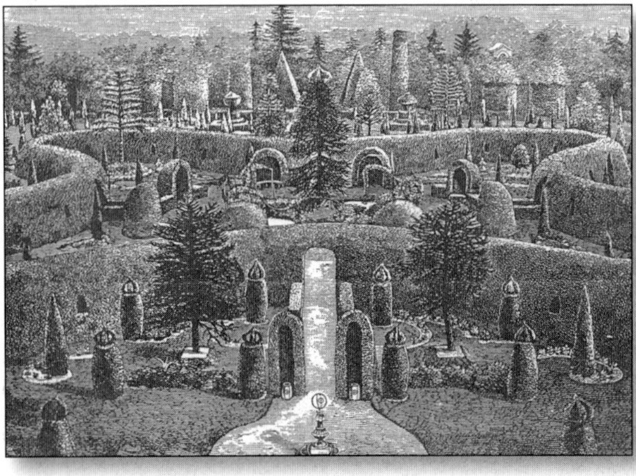

THE GARDEN, ELVASTON CASTLE

This extraordinary garden at Elvaston Castle in Derbyshire was the magnum opus of William Barron, the creator of Macclesfield's West Park. Different colours and foliage types of yew and holly were the main ingredients, plus a lot of clipping!

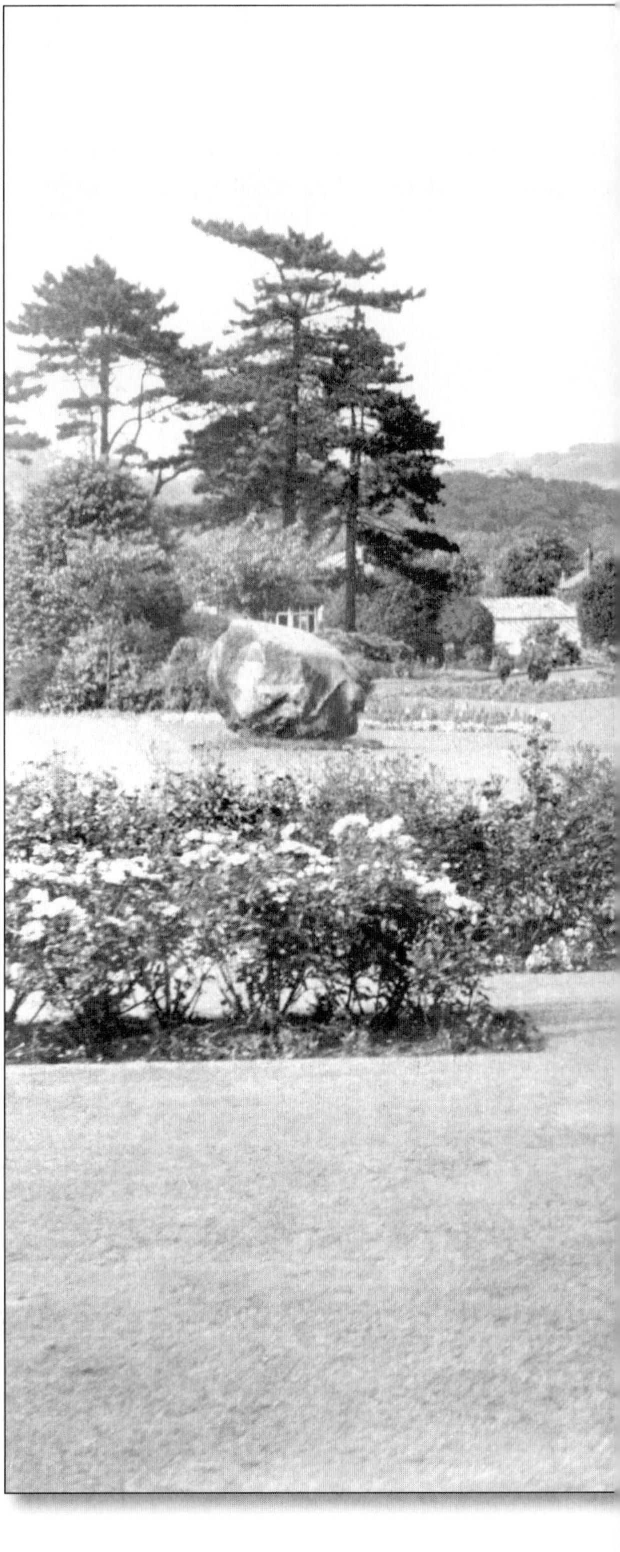

THE WEST END, PUBLIC WORKS AND JAMES STEVENS

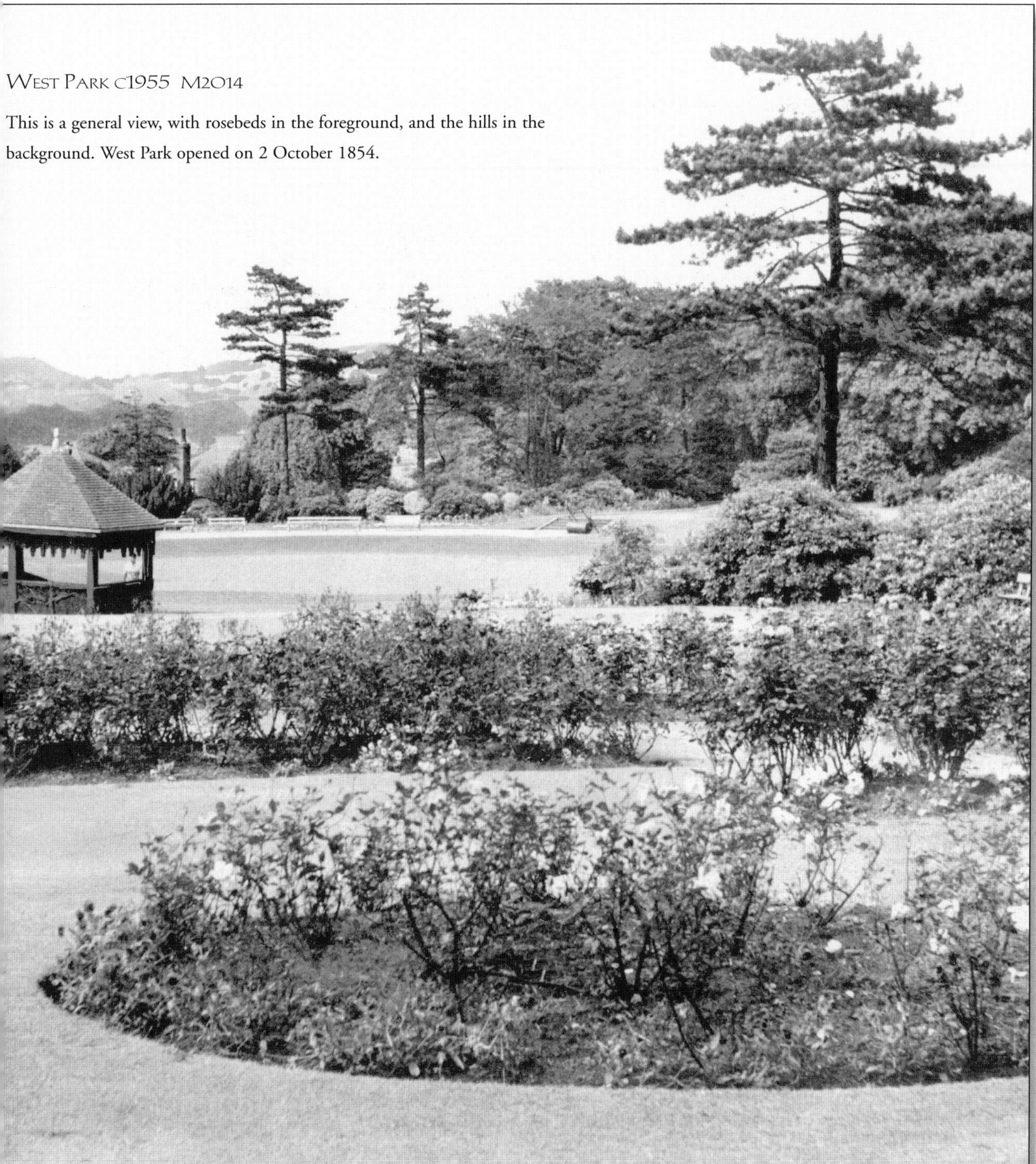

WEST PARK c1955 M2014

This is a general view, with rosebeds in the foreground, and the hills in the background. West Park opened on 2 October 1854.

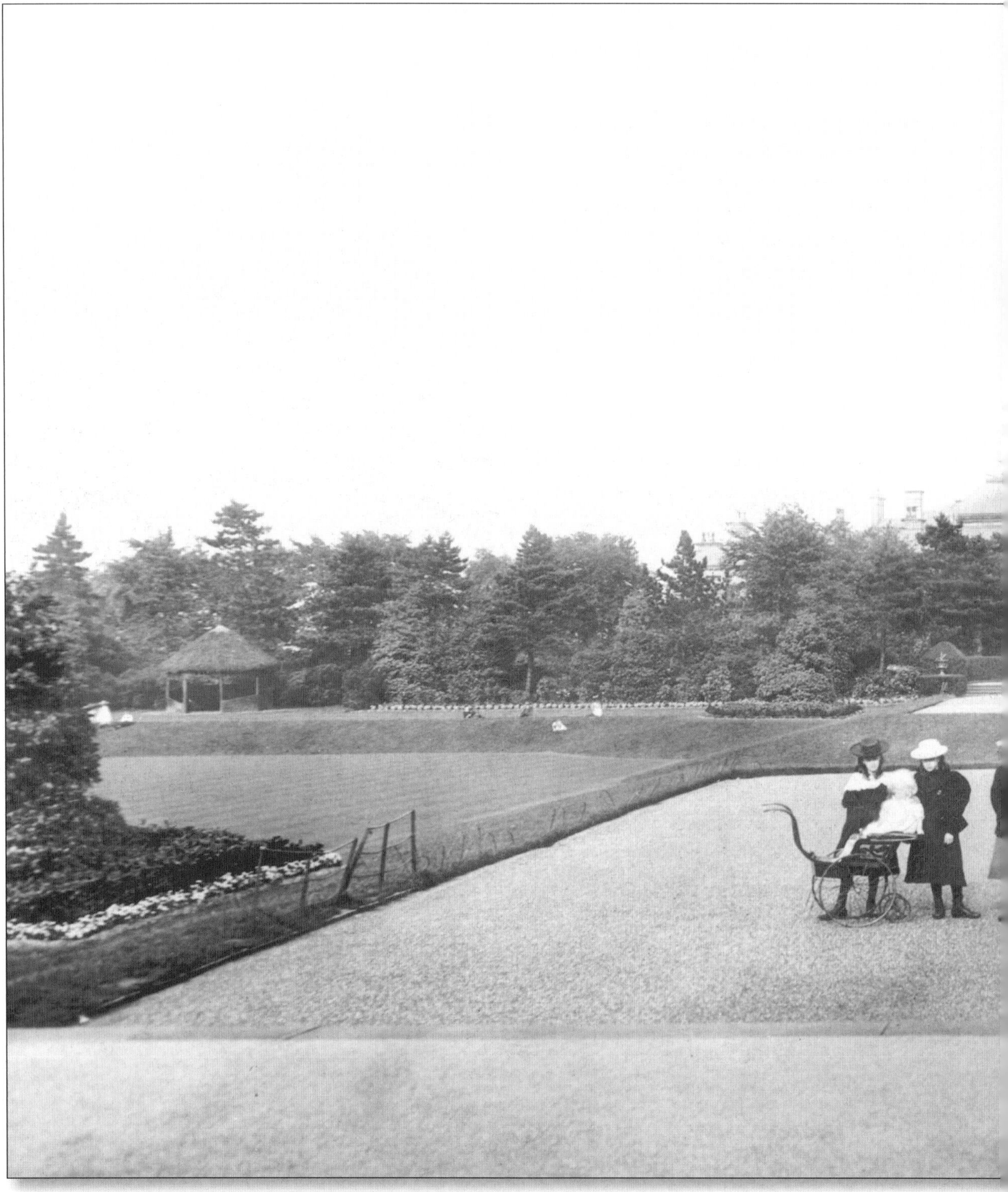

THE WEST END, PUBLIC WORKS AND JAMES STEVENS

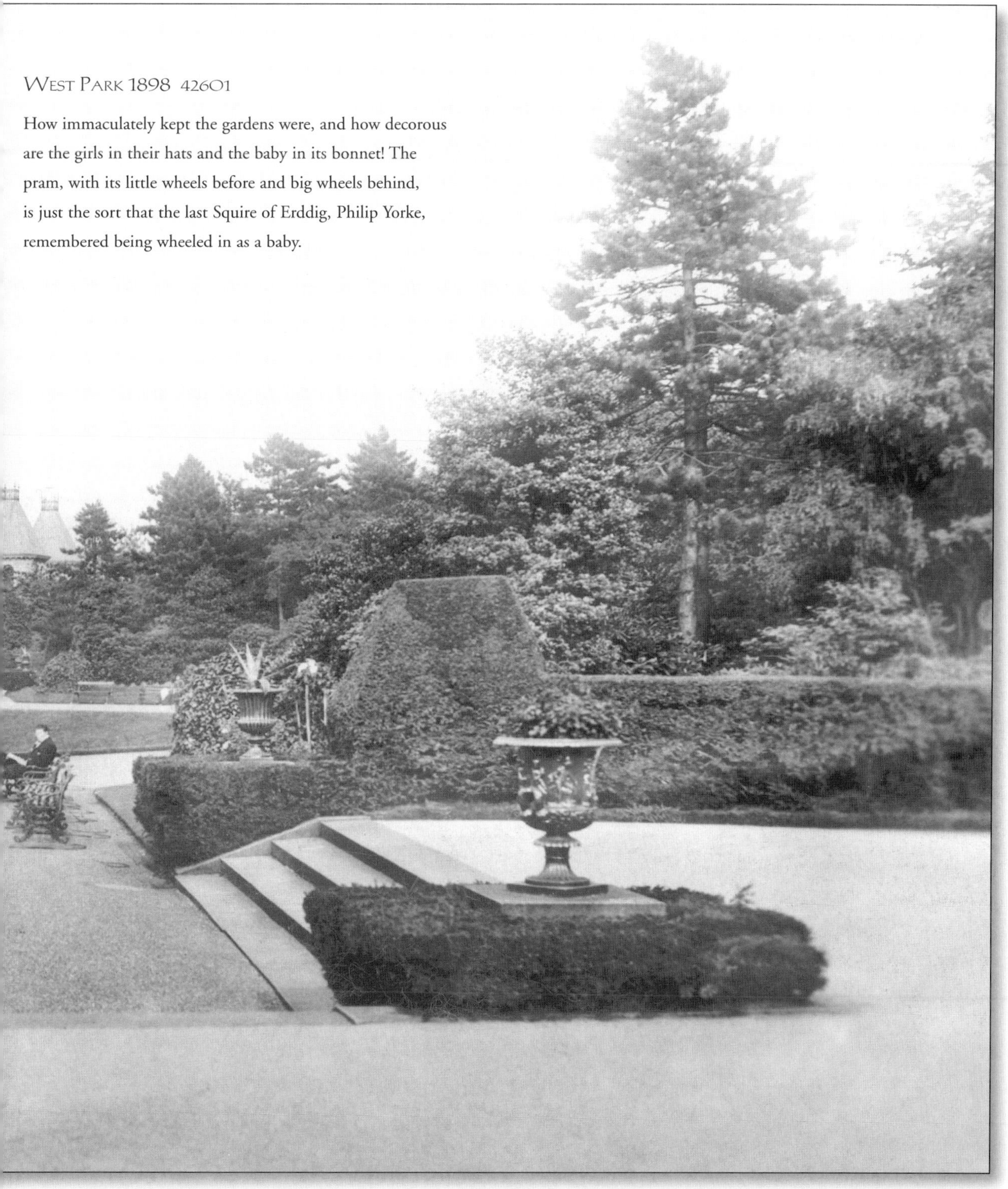

West Park 1898 42601

How immaculately kept the gardens were, and how decorous are the girls in their hats and the baby in its bonnet! The pram, with its little wheels before and big wheels behind, is just the sort that the last Squire of Erddig, Philip Yorke, remembered being wheeled in as a baby.

like 'Albertopolis' in South Kensington, where the line of symmetry runs right through from the Albert Memorial and Hall at one end to the Natural History Museum at the other). The central axis here runs right through from the clock tower through the main hall to the superintendent's house, with identical wards, infirmaries, airing grounds and the like on each side for male and female patients.

Parkside Hospital cost £141,823 in all. It was a complete world, with its own rules. It was self-sufficient even to its own farm, which was connected across Victoria Road by a bridge whose abutment can still be seen.

The hospital complex is built in a shiny red Ruabon brick, with yellow and blue bricks and some stone for contrast. It shows the influence of Ruskin's 'The Stones of Venice' which had appeared in 1851, advocating the use of built-in colour. There are a few houses here and there in town which show the same influence, and must be of the same date. Stylistically, Parkside is a mongrel affair, perhaps Italianate, perhaps Germanic, but decidedly Victorian. The asylum had a sizeable church as well, St Luke's, which was built of Teggsnose stone like the Infirmary. The author remembers singing Christmas carols there with the choir of St Paul's church.

Parkside was still expanding in the 1970s, and had 36 wards in operation with more than 1500 patients, but in the 1980s government policy came down heavily towards abolishing the huge mental hospitals in favour of integration and 'care in the community'. By 1995 there were only six wards in operation, and later in the same year the main building was closed altogether. The whole hospital was shut down by January 1997. Luckily it was not all demolished, as happened in some places, although some buildings have been lost. The site, a very favourable one, is now being extensively developed for housing.

Understandably, there is little attempt to commemorate the past. 'The Villas' and 'The Pavilions' are two names which have been retained, and the architectural style and colour of the new houses owes something to the surviving asylum buildings. The park-like landscape and many of the fine trees will survive too.

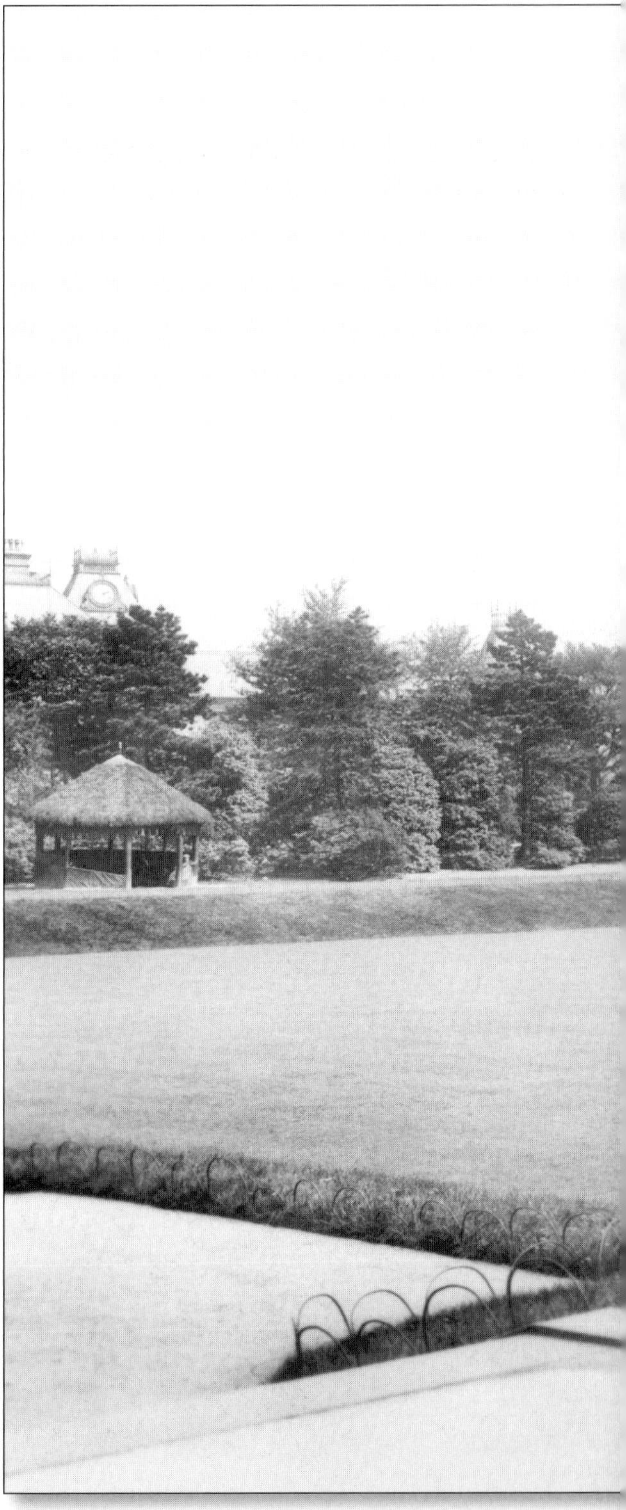

WEST PARK 1903 49467

The sunken Bowling Green has scalloped ends. In the background are the Infirmary (left), the spire of Trinity Chapel, and houses on Cumberland Street.

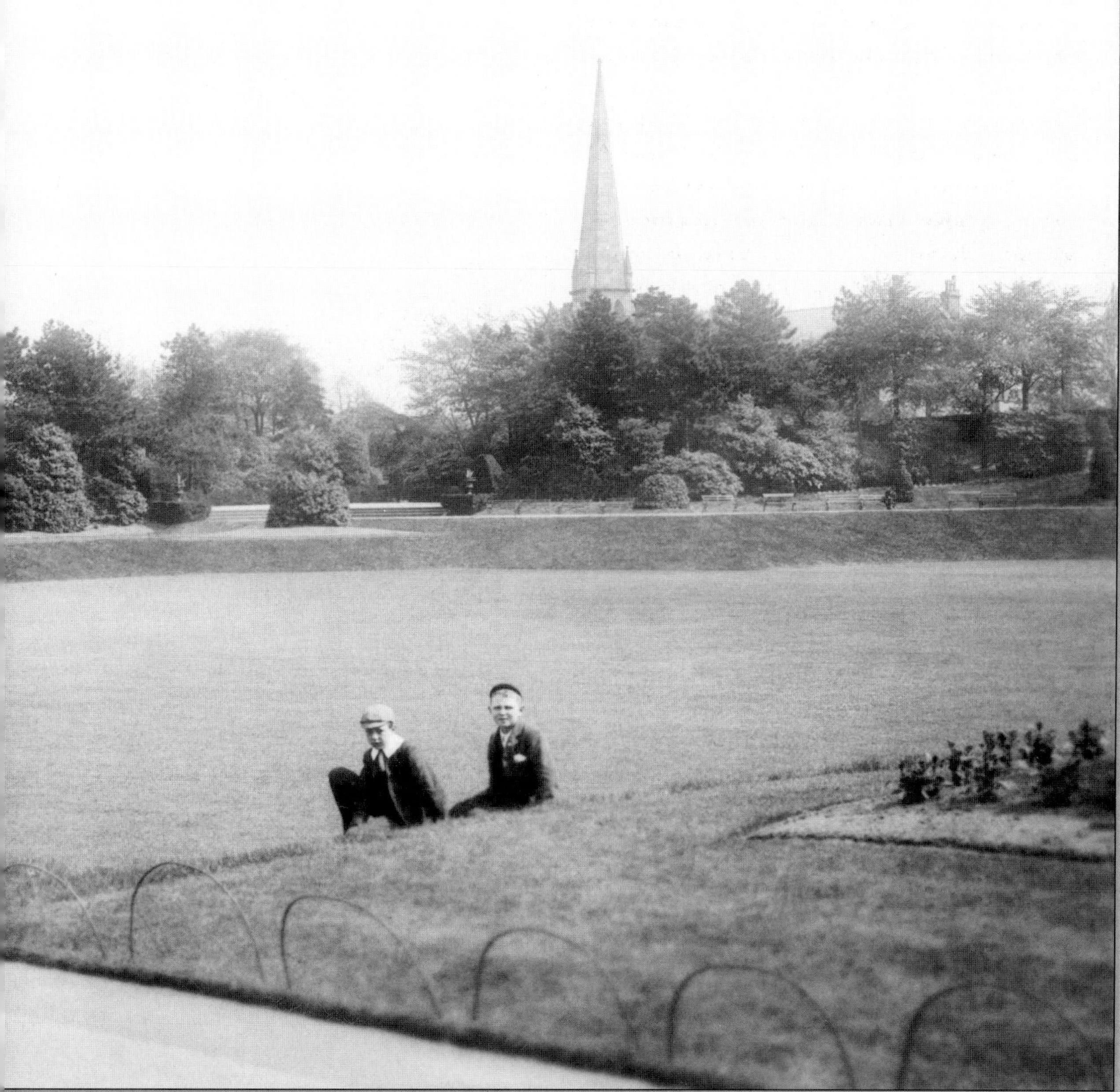

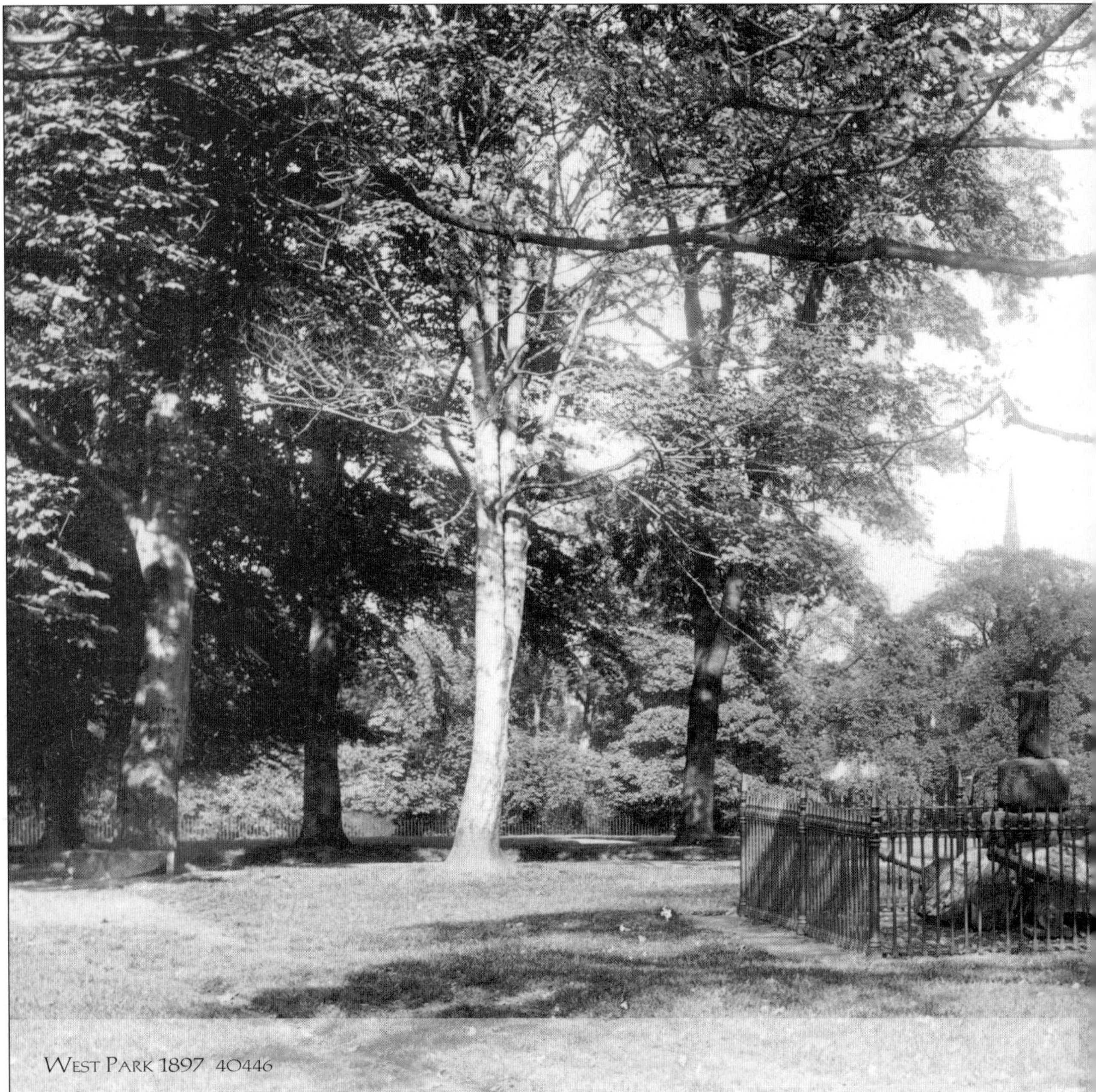

WEST PARK 1897 40446

This is the site of the adventure playground today. Behind railings is the Market Cross, which is now back in the Market Place - it has wandered about since the end of the 18th century. Two Russian cannon can just be seen as well; they were captured during the Crimean war at Sebastopol. The strange ancient stone pillar crosses are a local type. They do not belong here; two were brought from Ridge Farm, Wincle, the other from Upton. The slender spire of the cemetery chapel can be seen beyond.

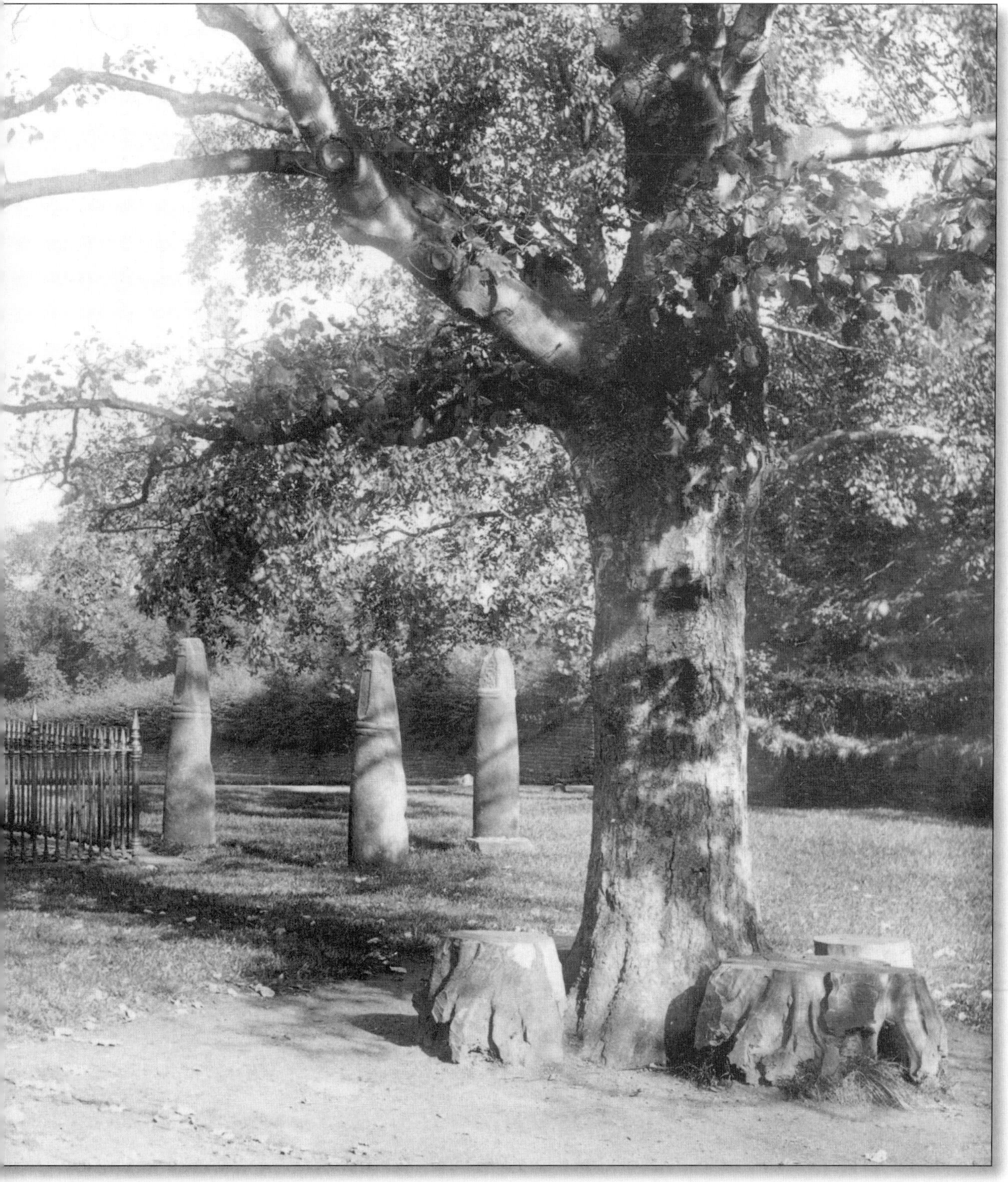

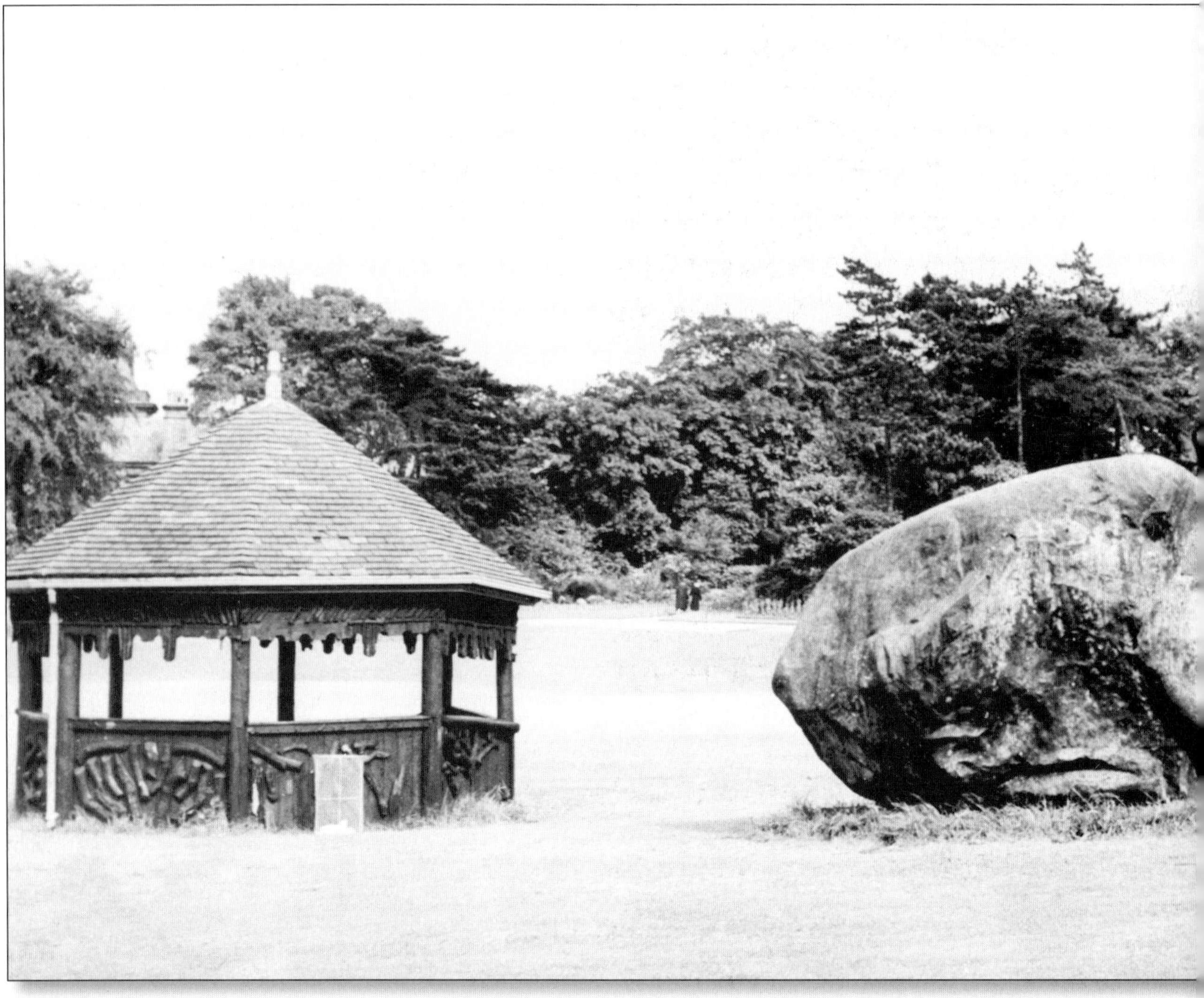

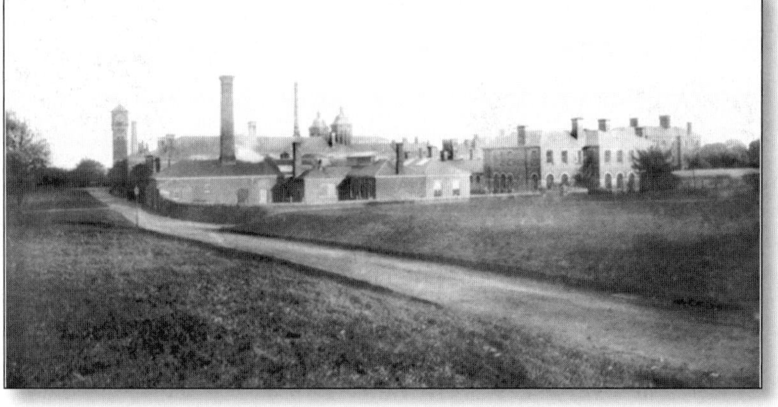

PARKSIDE ASYLUM 1897 40454

An unflattering general view. The laundry is in the foreground, the clocktower and main entrance are away on the left, and the female excited ward is to the right.

THE WEST END, PUBLIC WORKS AND JAMES STEVENS

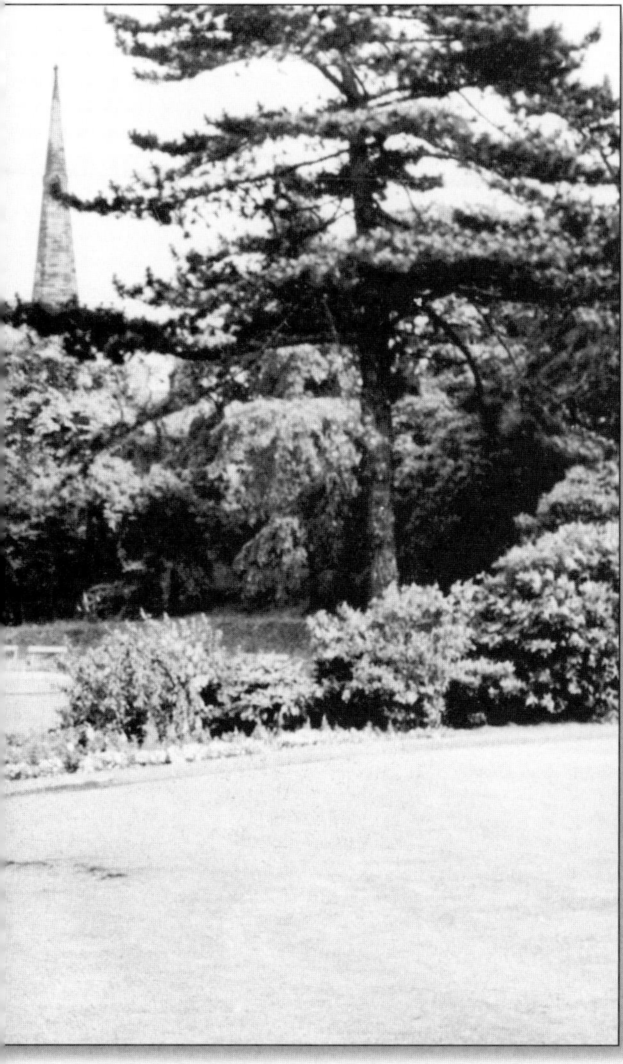

WEST PARK c1955 M2013

A 30-ton erratic boulder dominates the view. It was presented by Mr J H Beswick on 24 July 1857, having been found in a field next to Oxford Road. It must have been deposited there by a melting glacier during the last ice age. Lacking a handy glacier, how on earth did they move it from there to West Park? It can be seen that the rustic huts are now shingled, not thatched as they were originally. We can see the spire of Trinity Methodist in the distance.

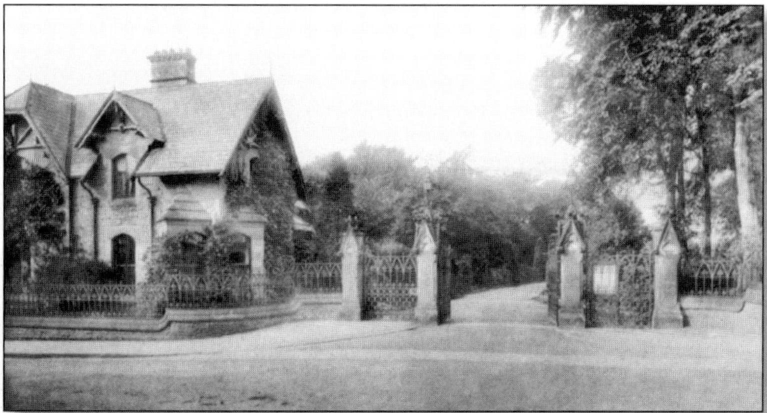

THE CEMETERY ENTRANCE 1898 42602

How complicated can you make a gateway and a lodge house? As with the cemetery chapels within, Mr Stevens seems to have added notches and frills and twiddly bits for their own sake. What's more, the whole composition, minus some of the finials, has survived complete.

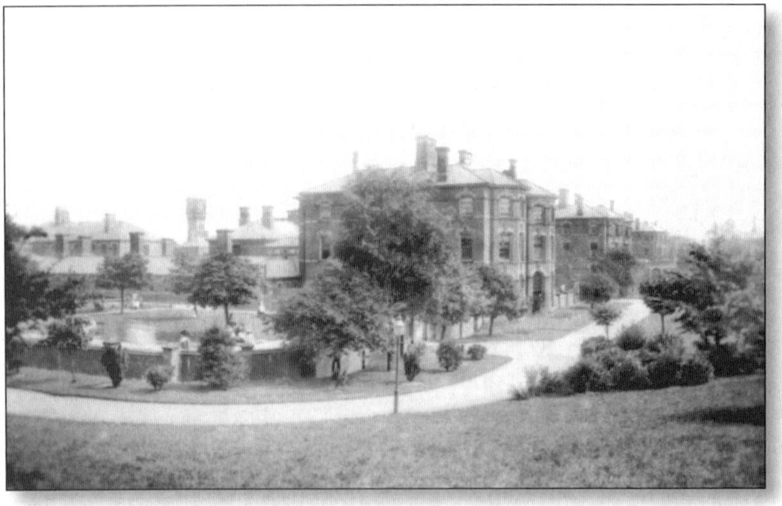

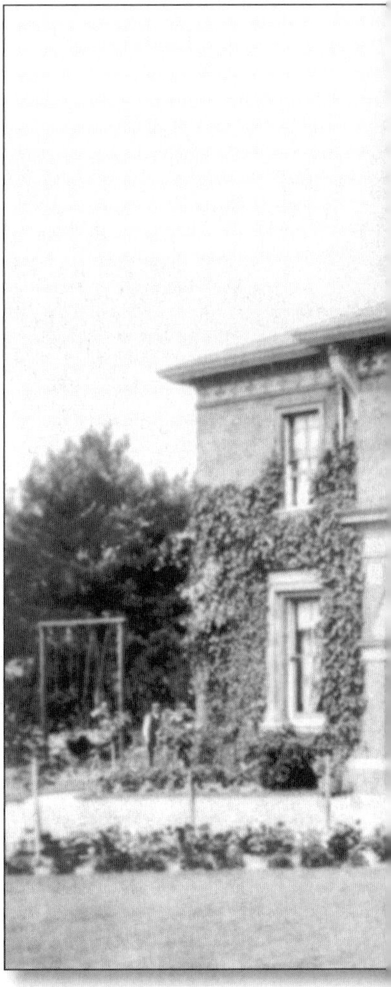

ABOVE: PARKSIDE ASYLUM 1898 42603

This fine photograph looks along the south front towards Chester Road. Four identical pavilions can be seen, stretching 912 feet in all. On the left is one of the airing or exercising grounds. It looks as though someone was going too fast for the camera!

BELOW: PARKSIDE ASYLUM, THE FEMALE WARDS 1898 42605

This is one of the four pavilions; the end of the dining hall and one of the water towers are behind. The park-like setting is well shown. These blocks are currently still standing derelict.

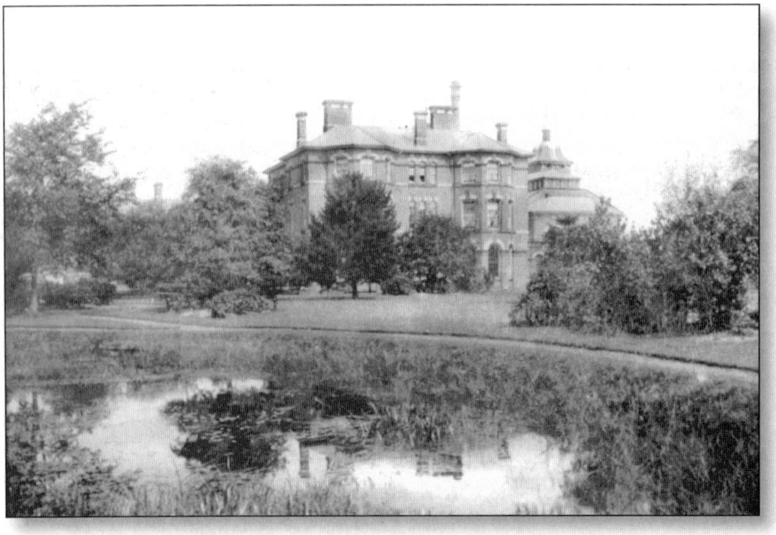

THE WEST END, PUBLIC WORKS AND JAMES STEVENS

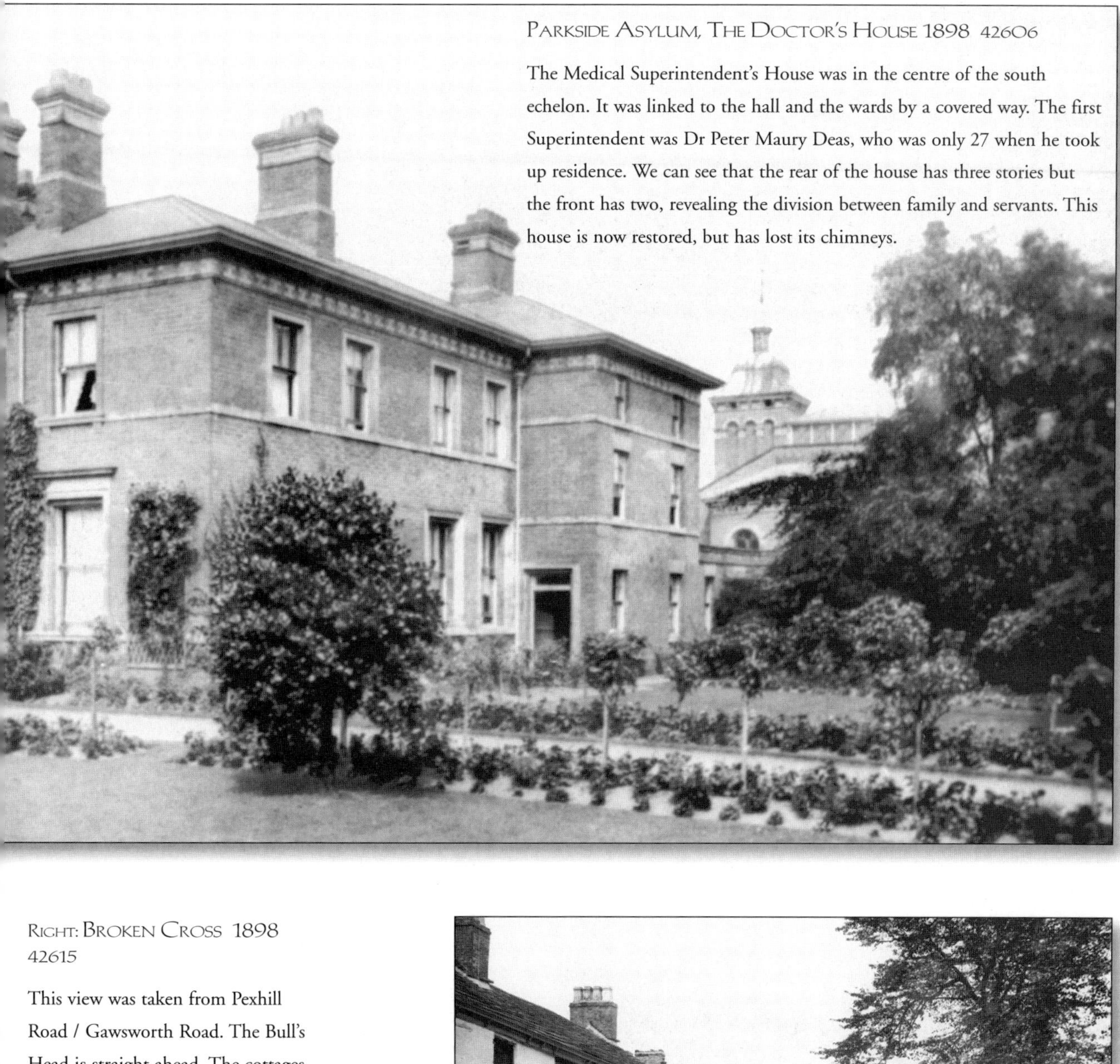

PARKSIDE ASYLUM, THE DOCTOR'S HOUSE 1898 42606

The Medical Superintendent's House was in the centre of the south echelon. It was linked to the hall and the wards by a covered way. The first Superintendent was Dr Peter Maury Deas, who was only 27 when he took up residence. We can see that the rear of the house has three stories but the front has two, revealing the division between family and servants. This house is now restored, but has lost its chimneys.

RIGHT: BROKEN CROSS 1898 42615

This view was taken from Pexhill Road / Gawsworth Road. The Bull's Head is straight ahead. The cottages today have all lost their whitewash, but a remnant can still be seen of the cobbled pavement. The nearest cottage is advertising 'Good accommodation for Cyclists'.

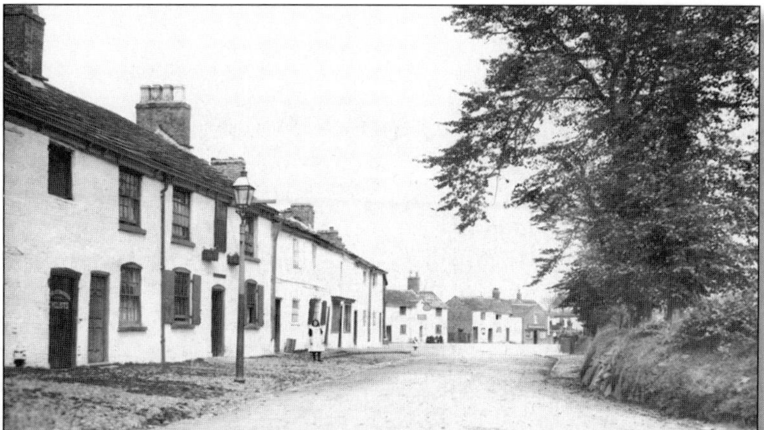

OUT INTO CHESHIRE

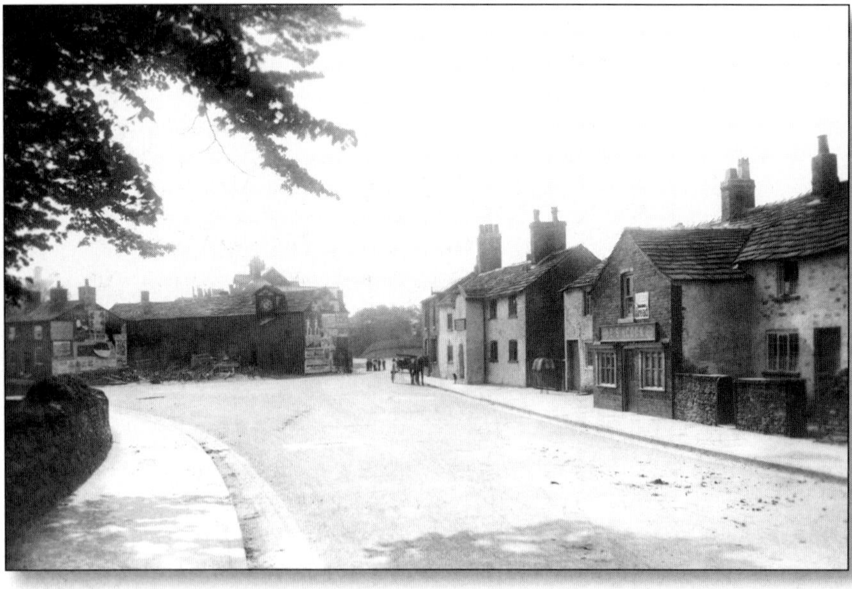

ABOVE: BROKEN CROSS 1903 49472

A peaceful scene compared with today. The photo shows the clock in its original position. Note all the agricultural machinery in front of it. Gable ends hereabouts are still used for advertising.

BELOW: HENBURY, THE CHURCH 1898 42614

This was built by Richard Lane in 1844-45. He lived at Oxford Lodge, Victoria Park, Manchester. Usually a classicist, this is one of his rare excursions into Gothic. The great Alfred Waterhouse trained under him, and so did Alfred Darbyshire, who was rather rude about his architectural talents.

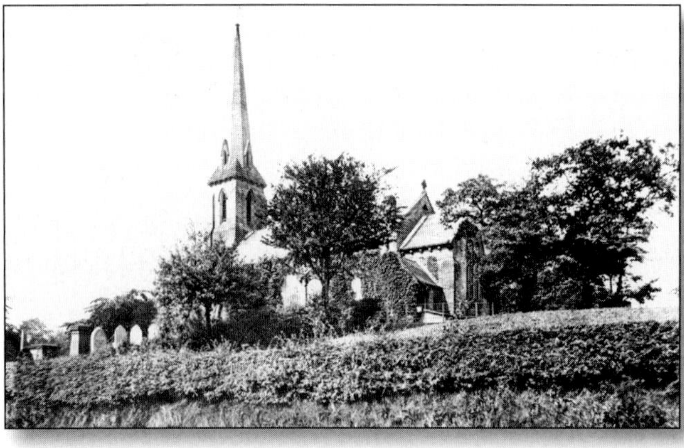

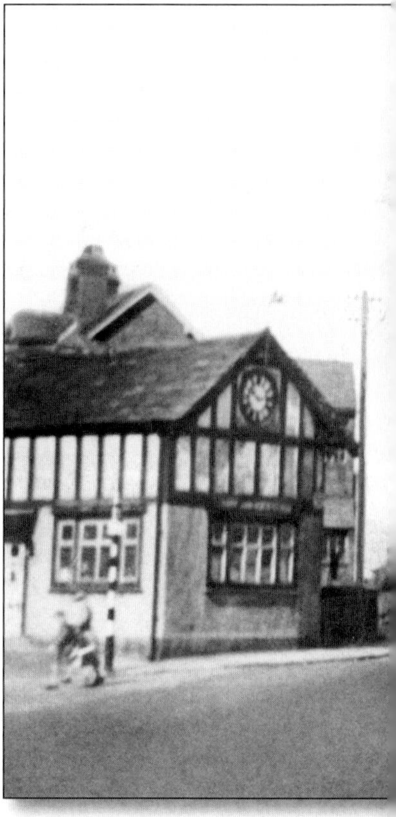

BROKEN CROSS c1955 M2001

There is still very little traffic. The clock had been moved when the building was altered for road widening. It was moved again across the road in 1988 to a new building immediately to the right of the Bull's Head. Fake timber-framing was obviously in fashion - compare this with 49472, above left. The Bull's Head has now reverted to its unadorned self.

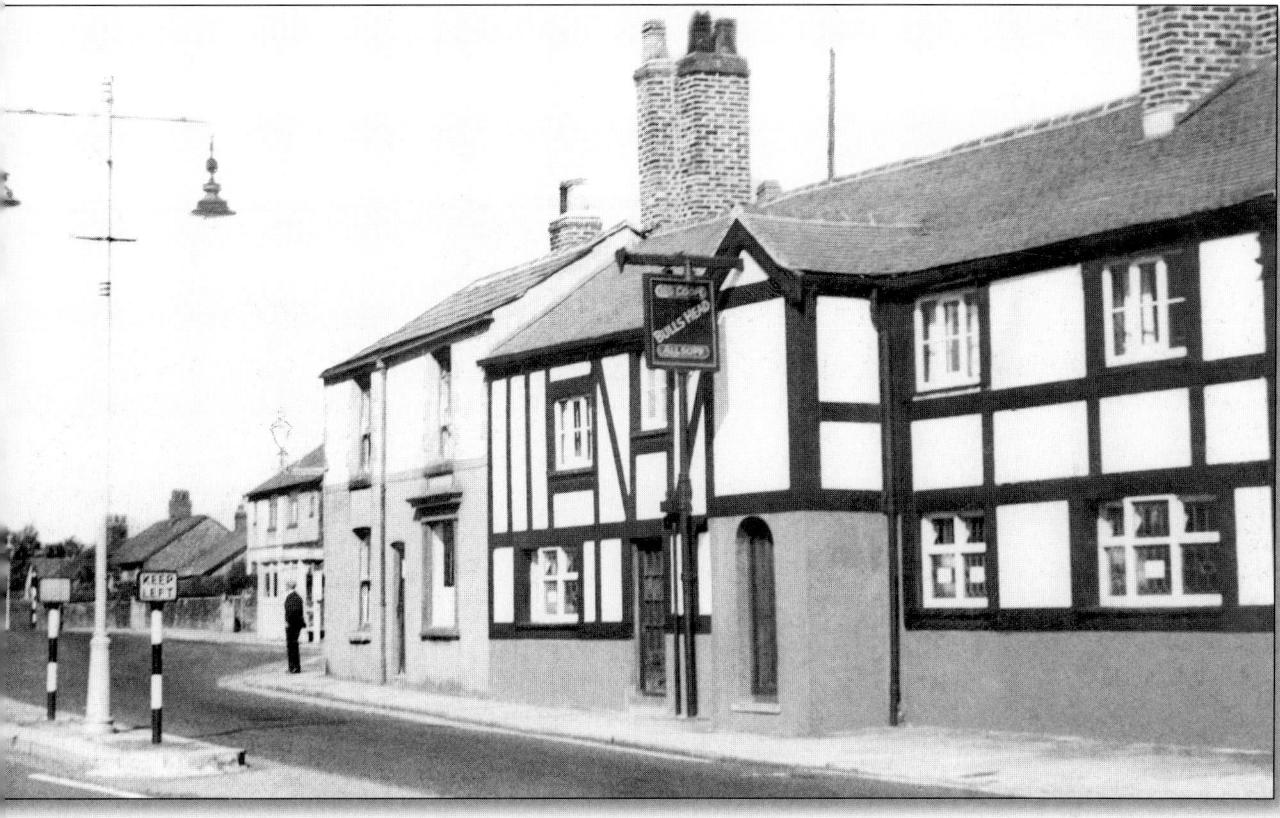

Broken Cross was the centre for blacksmiths and agricultural engineers. The well-known business of S & W Holland originated as a blacksmiths at the Bull's Head. The head of the firm, William Holland, was always known as 'Urgent' because everything had to be done in a hurry. He was also a crack shot and a keen cyclist. His shoes were always polished like chestnuts. His son Anthony very surprisingly became a successful designer of theatre costumes, dressing many West End shows. This unlikely choice of career from a farming and engineering business was paralleled and encouraged by Charles Tunnicliffe; coming from a similar background, he went on to be an artist of wildlife. Both talents were fostered by the Macclesfield School of Art.

A long straight mile beyond Broken Cross is the scattered village of Henbury, today remarkable for the beautiful but hidden Henbury Hall that was built by the Ferranti family as recently as 1984. The little church of St Thomas (42614, left) is well placed on a hillock above the Chester Road. Visitors to the Isle of Man might be surprised to see a near replica of St Thomas's, Henbury, by the mound of Tynwald where the annual parliament has been held for a thousand years. The two churches are indeed almost exactly the same, and are by the same architect, Richard Lane, but what the connection between Tynwald and Henbury may be is a mystery.

Birtles, set in pretty scenery on the by-road to Alderley, is scarcely even a hamlet. The church, St Catharine's (49463, page 80), was built by the Hibbert family of Birtles Hall in 1840 as a private chapel; it was very probably designed by Thomas Hibbert himself. It originated in a quarrel - a tale regrettably oft-repeated in church history - between Mr Hibbert and the Stanleys of Alderley, who refused to allow Mr Hibbert a private pew at St Mary's.

In 1890 the church, together with the site for a vicarage, were conveyed to the diocese as a parish church. The second Vicar, the Rev Henry Walden, wrote a fulsome description of the place in 1906. 'Certainly it is a fine prospect, this smiling sunny corner overlooking half Cheshire, with Birtles church embosomed in trees in the foreground. Few spots could be more lovely, and peaceful. Below a corner of Birtles Hall is seen,

OUT INTO CHESHIRE

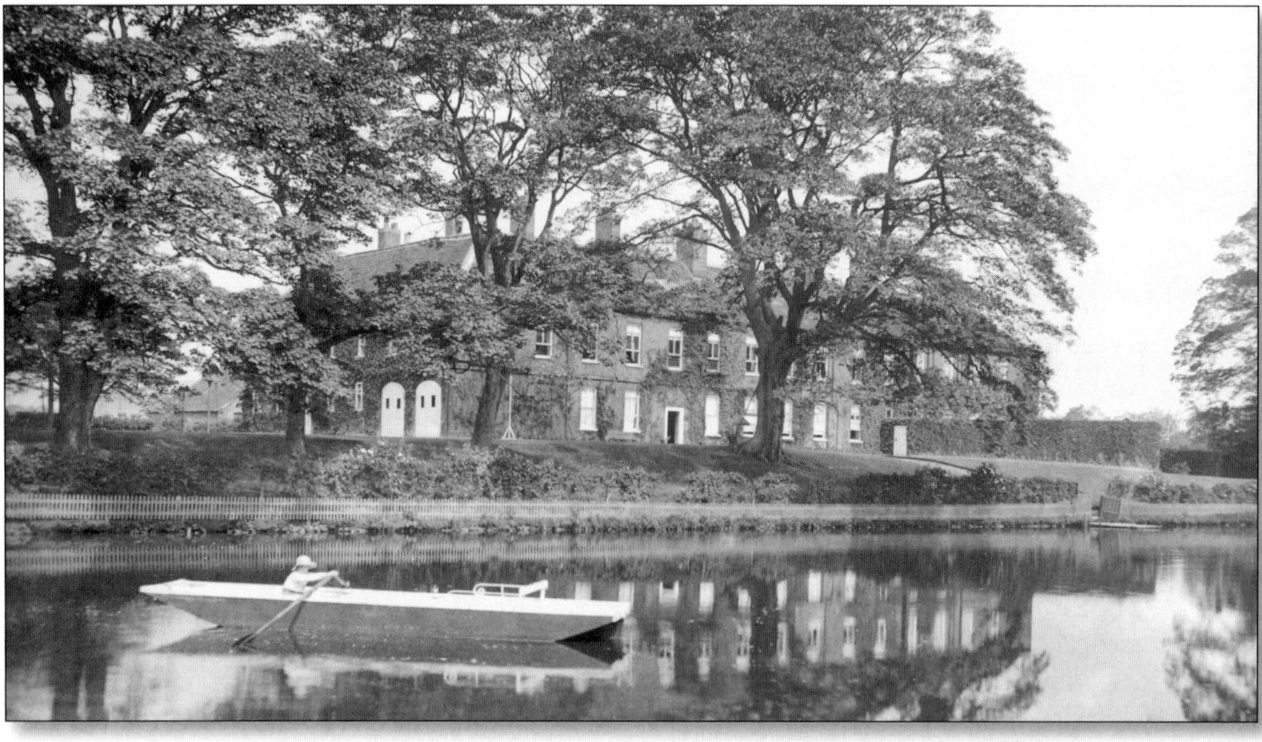

ABOVE: GAWSWORTH NEW HALL 1898 42609

It is difficult to see why these pictures were taken, except as a personal favour. The New Hall is a very plain building, although its setting by the topmost of a series of pools is fine. Lower down is the picturesque Old Hall, the beautiful church and the even more picturesque Old Rectory.

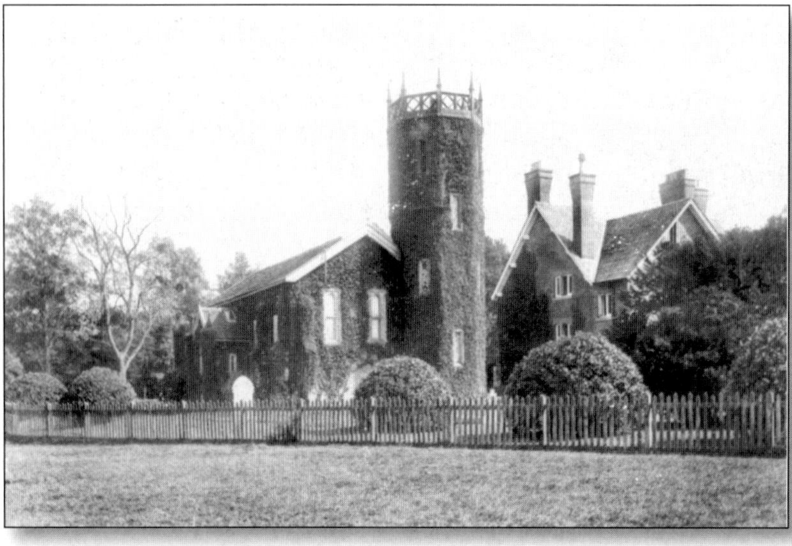

LEFT: BIRTLES, THE CHURCH 1903 49463

This little estate church was built in 1840. The initials TH and LHH which appear over the tower door and on the family pew stand for Thomas Hibbert and his sister Letitia Hamilton Hibbert, of Birtles Hall. It was, as can be seen, entirely covered with ivy 'neatly trimmed and cared for'. Today, inspecting architects would never allow this; there is just a little tasteful Virginia Creeper. The vicarage of 1892 is characteristically bigger than the church. A grave near the fence commemorates Harold and Mary Worth, killed by enemy action on 23 December 1940 at Acton Farm.

with its gardens and Scotch firs and rooks; indeed there are parts of the day when the air is suddenly alive with rooks, which come tumbling and wheeling in, flashing and chattering joyously in great clouds, as they separate themselves from their Astle and Capesthorne friends, and finally settle in the Birtles trees'.

23 December 1940 was the night of the Manchester Blitz. From Alderley and Birtles it was possible to see Manchester burning, the whole sky to the north lit up and lurid. A single bomber, perhaps crippled or short of fuel, dropped its bombs at random over Cheshire. One of them blew out a window of precious old glass at Birtles church. Another, by sheer chance, scored a direct hit on Acton Farm nearby. Three people were killed instantly. But when volunteers arrived to dig out the wreckage they found the two Worth children still alive, hidden under the kitchen table which had protected them from the collapsing house. Under a simple stone at the edge of the churchyard lie Harold and Mary Worth, killed by enemy action.

In 1830 almost the whole of continental Europe erupted in revolt, a continuation of what had started in France in the revolution of 1789. One result of this was the creation of the state of Belgium. Another was the sudden availablity of quantities of old stained glass, antique carved wood and decorative metal from the sacked monasteries of the Low Countries. Thomas Hibbert of Birtles was aware of this, and commissioned an agent on the continent to pick up what he could for his intended new church. The result is a cleverly assembled kaleidoscope of pieces bearing different dates and different languages. Although it creates a very rich impression, it tells us nothing of Cheshire history; but it is unintentionally revealing of the nouveau-riche Hibberts' desire to a acquire a history of their own.

A diversion to the south will take us to the picturebook village of Gawsworth, with its pools, old trees, venerable houses, fine church, waterfowl, and rooks. The Old Hall and the Old Rectory are wonderful specimens of Cheshire timber framing. The New Hall (42609, left and 42610, page 82) is dull in comparison; the only remarkable thing is that building operations were stopped by the famous duel fought in 1712 between Lord Mohun of Gawsworth and his cousin the Duke of Hamilton, in which both partners were killed. The great barn was built by the Earl of Harrington in about 1745, hence the Harrington Arms at the far end of the village. Perhaps this is the connection with Macclesfield that led a later Lord Harrington to allow his head gardener, William Barron, to design West Park.

Gawsworth church, with its tall pinnacled tower reflected in the still waters of the pool, is one of the finest of Cheshire churches. But it is also very unusual, because the body of the church is so wide and so low, with no aisles and no chancel arch. This has the effect of making the tower seem unusually tall, and means that the interior is effectively a single room. There is a fine array of Elizabethan and Jacobean monuments to the Fitton family of Gawsworth in the chancel.

RIGHT: BIRTLES, THE CHURCH, THE INTERIOR 1903 49464

After the plain exterior of the church, the interior is a bit of a shock. It is astonishingly ornate, and was even more so before Colonel Hugh Hibbert's wall painting was whitewashed over. The church is stuffed with old woodwork, brass, and stained glass, all of it imported from the continent. On the left is the Hibbert's family pew, much more magnificent than that of the Stanleys at Alderley, and by virtue of its old woodwork and glass, older too!

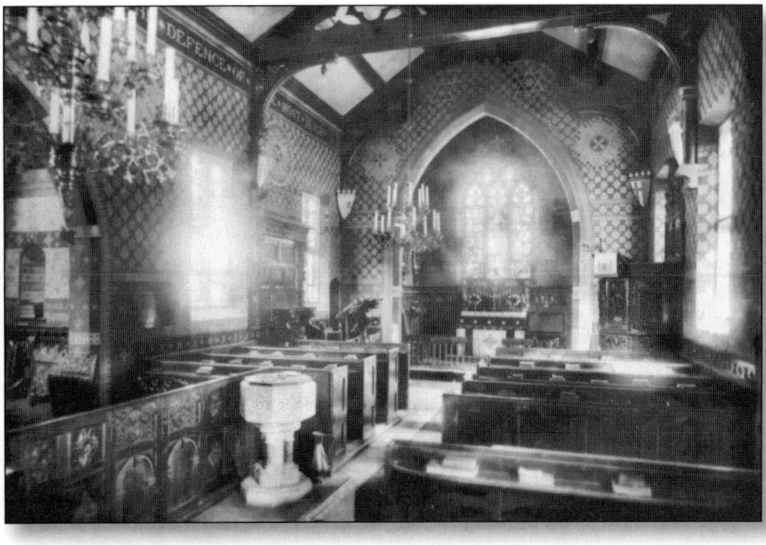

OUT INTO CHESHIRE

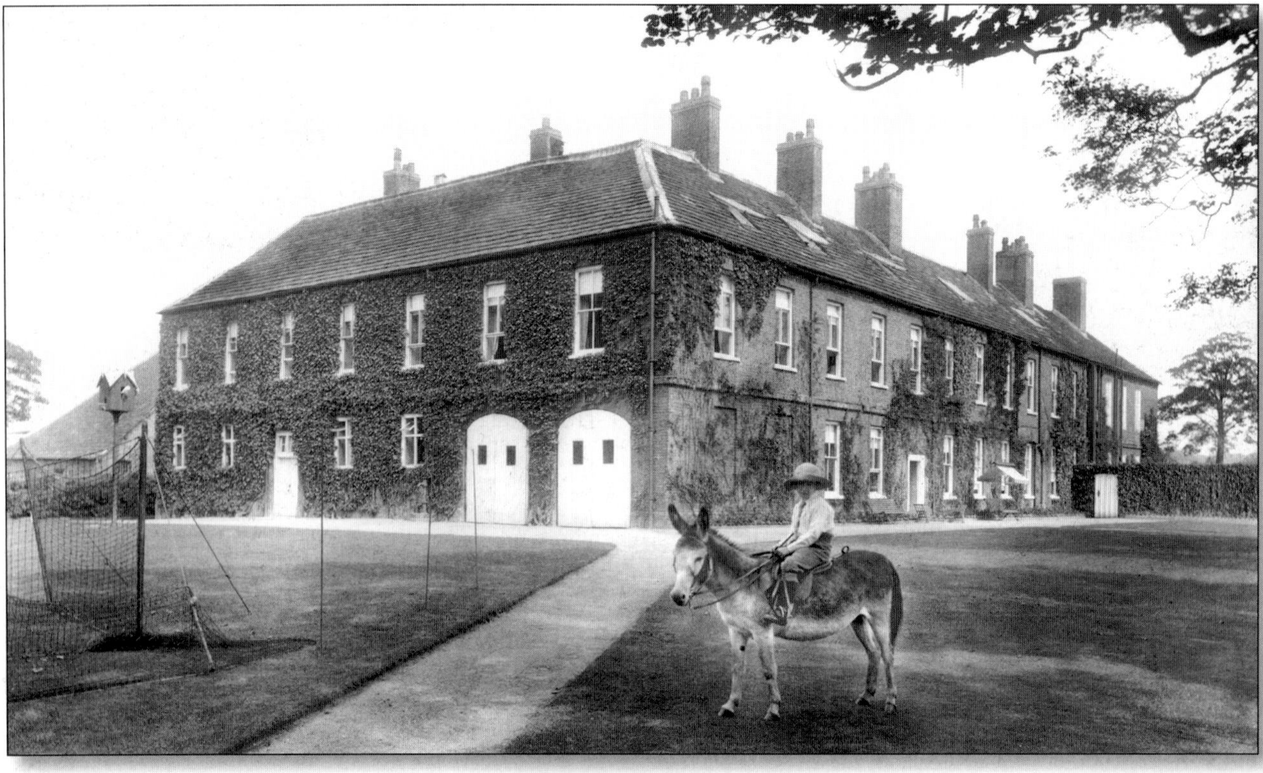

ABOVE:
GAWSWORTH, NEW HALL 1898 42610

A leisurely country scene; note the lawn set out for games, and the swinging seat under its canopy. Behind the bird house on the left is a wonderful great barn with a sweeping roof of Kerridge stone slabs. The hall itself has now lost its stable doors, and the ivy, and has acquired a fine central doorcase complete with the Harrington arms.

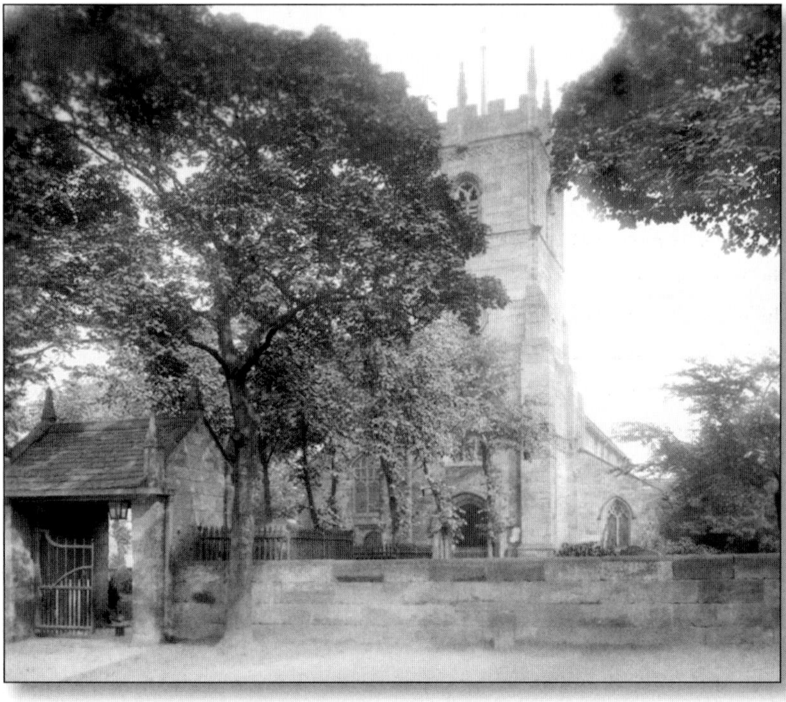

RIGHT:
PRESTBURY, THE CHURCH 1898 42616

The photographer stood by the unique timber-framed priest's house across the road to take this. It shows the homely lych gate of 1728 and the fine 15th-century tower, and hints at the huge and very beautiful churchyard that is the real glory of Prestbury.

OUT INTO CHESHIRE

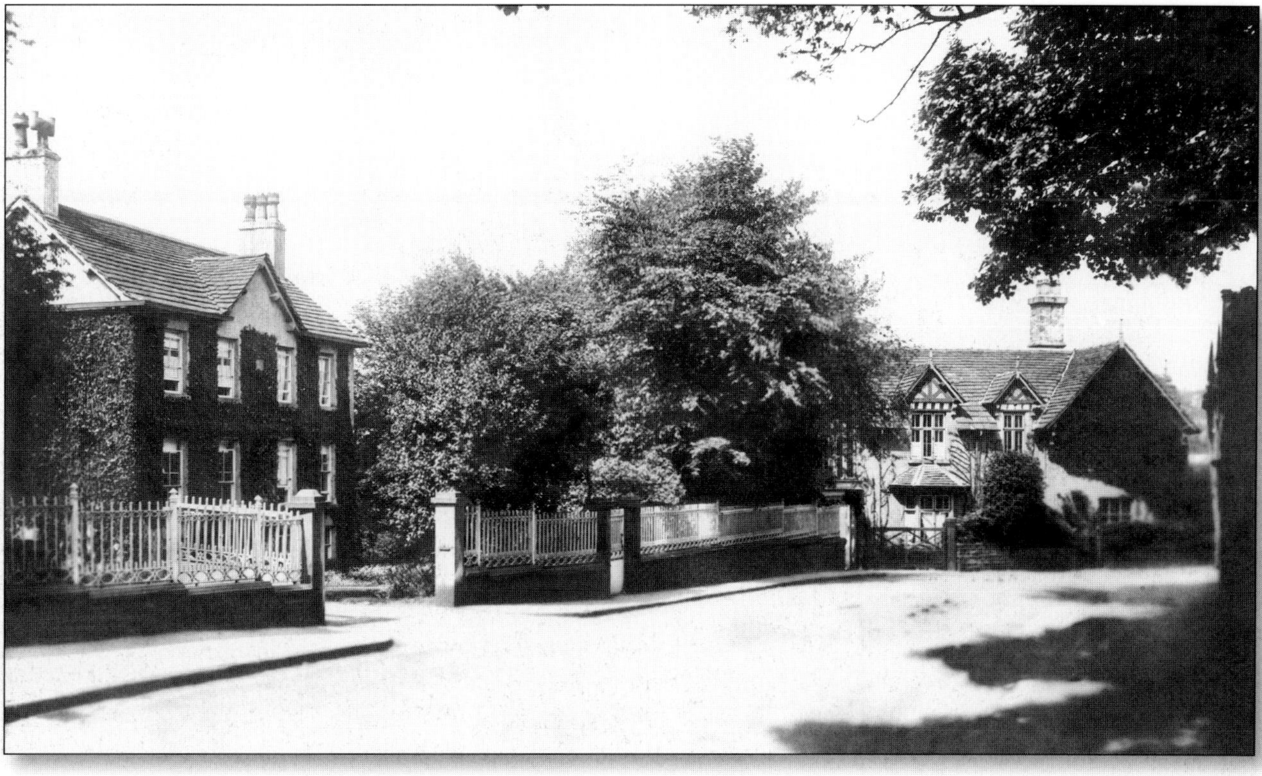

PRESTBURY, THE MANOR HOUSE 1903 49474

Prestbury is an especially handsome village, although greatly overgrown and gentrified today. The Bollin runs through the village, passing the side of the churchyard and under the main street where it dips down to the right.

We end where we should have started. Prestbury (42616, left) was the mother church of Macclesfield. Its ancient parish, one of the largest in the country, stretched right up to Rainow and Kettleshulme in the hills, north as far as Poynton, and out in the south and west to Bosley and Chelford. Macclesfield town was in the parish of Prestbury until the 19th century, although it had long outgrown its parent. A walk round Prestbury churchyard (especially recommended in crocus time) will leave an outstanding impression of the antiquity of the place, as evidenced by the carved Saxon cross and the little Norman chapel that stand near the church, and of the sheer size of the graveyard which is a reflection of the size of the parish. The windows of the Norman chapel at Prestbury are glazed with a delightful modern series of pictures relating to the following poem:

When as a child I laughed and wept,
time crept.
When as a youth I dreamed and talked,
time walked.
When I became a full-grown man, time ran.
And later as I older grew, time flew.
Soon I shall find while travelling on,
time gone.
Will Christ have saved my soul by then? Amen.

This seems a good note on which to finish this book.

Names of Pre-Publication Buyers

The following people have kindly supported this book by purchasing limited edition copies prior to publication.

The Baguley Family, Macclesfield
In memory of Mary Barber, Henbury
Kenneth A Barrow
Mary Barrow
Happy Fathers Day Barry love Julie xxx
Roy Bettany for Christmas 2005
Sheila Birchenough (nee Barnett), Jodrell St
The late Ferdinand M Bonnaud, Macclesfield
The Bowers Family, Macclesfield
Peter Bryant, Macclesfield
In memory of Mr & Mrs A Burgoyne, Macclesfield
In memory of Eric Cawley, Macclesfield
Hedley Cooper, Macclesfield
Mr C Daly & daughter Josephine
Jonathan Dawes, admitted to the Roll of Solicitors August 2005
Michelle Dawes, lest you forget, love Mum and Dad x
Remembered, Lilian May Fordham, Macclesfield
Alice Fountain
Mr Wayne Francis & Mrs Lindsay Francis
Suzanne Del Frate, Macclesfield
David C Gosling, Macclesfield
Mr & Mrs R Greenwood, in memory of Roy Greenwood
To Nicky Hutchings from her son Jack
Mrs A M Jackson (nee Clulow), Macclesfield
Kathleen & Philip James, Macclesfield
To Bob Jenner, Happy Birthday, Mum 28/02/05
Philip Nemmy Jones, 'old stag on his 60th'
Mr John Trevor Kearns, Macclesfield
Mrs Marjorie Kearns, Macclesfield
Brian Kemp, Macclesfield
In memory of Mr & Mrs W H Leonard, Macclesfield
The Lomas Family, Macclesfield
Macclesfield Express
The Mannion Family, Macclesfield
Mr J Miller & Mr D Miller, Macclesfield
Colin & Pennie Molloy, Macclesfield
The Moorcroft Family, Macclesfield
Dorothy Mylan
In memory of Keneth & Elsie Neale, Macclesfield
Robert Keneth Neale
As a tribute to my loving parents, Patricia
Mr J E & Mrs A Pike
David Michael Pointon from Macclesfield
Family Pritchard, Macclesfield
The Puddle Family, Macclesfield
Tony & Joyce Robinson, Macclesfield
Kimberley Sellars, Macclesfield
Mr A R & Mrs S Sharp, Macclesfield
Mr R Skirvin, Macclesfield
Amy & the late Harold Stacey, Vivien & Valerie
The Stubbs Family, Macclesfield
In memory of John Stubbs, Macclesfield
Barry Swindells
In memory of Ron Tomkinson, Macclesfield
D Ulpis & V Ulpiene, Macclesfield
In memory of Harold & Annie Varty from Helen, Ruth & Jane
The Vernon Family, Macclesfield
Ella Warne
Emma Warne
George Warne
Robert George West, Macclesfield
Frank & Betty Whittingham - Golden Wedding
To Dennis Whyte, 'Happy 70th' love from the kids
Vera Wilkinson
Elaine Wilson, Macclesfield
Kate Wilson, born in Macclesfield 16/03/1965
In memory of Brenda Woolley 1921-2005

INDEX

The 108 Steps........ 21
Barracks........ 62-63
Birtles Church........ 80, 81
Brocklehurst Almshouses........ 20
Broken Cross........ 76-77, 78-79
Buxton Road........ 14-15, 16-17
Cat and Fiddle........ 10-11, 12-13
Cemetery Entrance........ 75
Chestergate........ 32-33
Christchurch........ 46-47
Churchwallgate........ 30
Elvaston Castle Garden........ 66
The Fence or Brocklehurst Almshouses........ 20
Free Library........ 38, 64
Gawsworth New Hall........ 80, 82
Henbury Church........ 57, 78
Hurdsfield Church........ 51
Infirmary........ 64-65
Market Place........ 24-25, 27
Mill Street........ 31
Parish Church........ 8-9, 26
Park Green........ 34-35, 36-37, 38-39, 44-45, 56-57
Park Green and the Cenotaph........ 40-41, 42-43
Parkside Asylum........ 74, 76-77
Prestbury Church........ 82
Prestbury Manor House........ 83
St Albans Church........ 50
St James's Church........ 52-53
St Paul's Church........ 54
St Peter's Church........ 54-55
Sunday School........ 47
Town Hall........ 60-61
Victoria Park........ 18-19, 20-21
Wesleyan Trinity Chapel........ 57
West Park........ 2, 66-67, 68-69, 70-71, 72-73, 74-75

The Francis Frith Collection Titles (continued)

Lancaster, Morecombe and Heysham Pocket Album
Leeds PA
Leicester
Leicestershire
Lincolnshire Living Memoires
Lincolnshire Pocket Album
Liverpool and Merseyside
London PA
Ludlow
Maidenhead
Maidstone
Malmesbury
Manchester PA
Marlborough
Matlock
Merseyside Living Memories
Nantwich and Crewe
New Forest
Newbury Living Memories
Newquay to St Ives
North Devon Living Memories
North London
North Wales
North Yorkshire
Northamptonshire
Northumberland
Northwich
Nottingham
Nottinghamshire PA
Oakham
Odiham Then and Now
Oxford Pocket Album
Oxfordshire
Padstow
Pembrokeshire
Penzance
Petersfield Then and Now
Plymouth
Poole and Sandbanks
Preston PA
Ramsgate Old and New
Reading Pocket Album
Redditch Living Memories
Redhill to Reigate
Rhondda Valley Living Mems
Richmond
Ringwood
Rochdale
Romford PA
Salisbury PA
Scotland
Scottish Castles
Sevenoaks and Tonbridge
Sheffield and South Yorkshire PA
Shropshire
Somerset
South Devon Coast
South Devon Living Memories
South East London
Southampton PA
Southend PA
Southport
Southwold to Aldeburgh
Stourbridge Living Memories
Stratford upon Avon
Stroud
Suffolk
Suffolk PA
Surrey Living Memories
Sussex
Sutton
Swanage and Purbeck
Swansea Pocket Album
Swindon Living Memories
Taunton
Teignmouth
Tenby and Saundersfoot
Tiverton
Torbay
Truro
Uppingham
Villages of Kent
Villages of Surrey
Villages of Sussex PA
Wakefield and the Five Towns Living Memories
Warrington
Warwick
Warwickshire PA
Wellingborough Living Memories
Wells
Welsh Castles
West Midlands PA
West Wiltshire Towns
West Yorkshire
Weston-super-Mare
Weymouth
Widnes and Runcorn
Wiltshire Churches
Wiltshire Living memories
Wiltshire PA
Wimborne
Winchester PA
Windermere
Windsor
Wirral
Wokingham and Bracknell
Woodbridge
Worcester
Worcestershire
Worcestershire Living Memories
Wyre Forest
York PA
Yorkshire
Yorkshire Coastal Memories
Yorkshire Dales
Yorkshire Revisited

FRITH PRODUCTS & SERVICES

Francis Frith would doubtless be pleased to know that the pioneering publishing venture he started in 1860 still continues today. Over a hundred and forty years later, The Francis Frith Collection continues in the same innovative tradition and is now one of the foremost publishers of vintage photographs in the world. Some of the current activities include:

Interior Decoration

Today Frith's photographs can be seen framed and as giant wall murals in thousands of pubs, restaurants, hotels, banks, retail stores and other public buildings throughout the country. In every case they enhance the unique local atmosphere of the places they depict and provide reminders of gentler days in an increasingly busy and frenetic world.

Product Promotions

Frith products are used by many major companies to promote the sales of their own products or to reinforce their own history and heritage. Frith promotions have been used by Hovis bread, Courage beers, Scots Porage Oats, Colman's mustard, Cadbury's foods, Mellow Birds coffee, Dunhill pipe tobacco, Guinness, and Bulmer's Cider.

Genealogy and Family History

As the interest in family history and roots grows world-wide, more and more people are turning to Frith's photographs of Great Britain for images of the towns, villages and streets where their ancestors lived; and, of course, photographs of the churches and chapels where their ancestors were christened, married and buried are an essential part of every genealogy tree and family album.

Frith Products

All Frith photographs are available Framed or just as Mounted Prints and Posters (size 23 x 16 inches). These may be ordered from the address below. From time to time other products - Address Books, Calendars, Table Mats, etc - are available.

The Internet

Already ninety thousand Frith photographs can be viewed and purchased on the internet through the Frith websites and a myriad of partner sites.

For more detailed information on Frith companies and products, look at these sites:

www.francisfrith.co.uk
www.francisfrith.com
(for North American visitors)

See the complete list of Frith Books at:
www.francisfrith.co.uk
This web site is regularly updated with the latest list of publications from The Francis Frith Collection. If you wish to buy books relating to another part of the country that your local bookshop does not stock, you may purchase on-line.

For further information, trade, or author enquiries please contact us at the address below:
The Francis Frith Collection, Frith's Barn, Teffont, Salisbury, Wiltshire, England SP3 5QP.
Tel: +44 (0)1722 716 376 Fax: +44 (0)1722 716 881 Email: sales@francisfrith.co.uk

See Frith books on the internet at www.francisfrith.co.uk

FREE PRINT OF
FREE PRINT OF
YOUR CHOICE

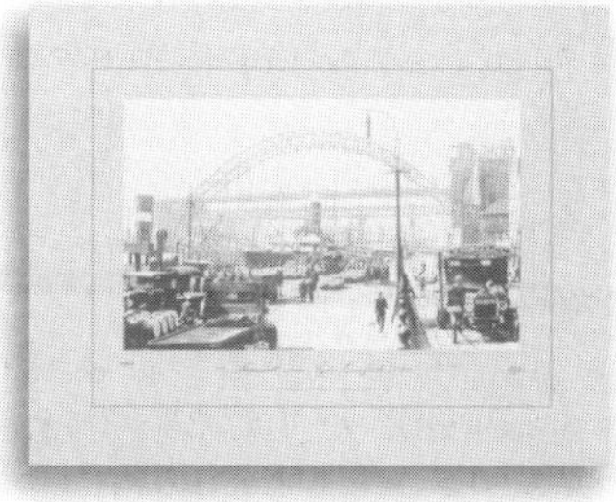

Mounted Print
Overall size 14 x 11 inches (355 x 280mm)

Choose any Frith photograph in this book. Simply complete the Voucher opposite and return it with your remittance for £2.25 (to cover postage and handling) and we will print the photograph of your choice in SEPIA (size 11 x 8 inches) and supply it in a cream mount with a burgundy rule line (overall size 14 x 11 inches). **Please note: photographs with a reference number starting with a "Z" are not Frith photographs and cannot be supplied under this offer.**
Offer valid for delivery to one UK address only.

***PLUS:* Order additional Mounted Prints at HALF PRICE - £7.49 each** (normally £14.99)
If you would like to order more Frith prints from this book, possibly as gifts for friends and family, you can buy them at half price (with no additional postage and handling costs).

***PLUS:* Have your Mounted Prints framed**
For an extra £14.95 per print you can have your mounted print(s) framed in an elegant polished wood and gilt moulding, overall size 16 x 13 inches (no additional postage and handling required).

IMPORTANT!

These special prices are only available if you use this form to order. You must use the ORIGINAL VOUCHER on this page (no copies permitted). We can only despatch to one UK address. This offer cannot be combined with any other offer.

Send completed Voucher form to:
The Francis Frith Collection, Frith's Barn, Teffont, Salisbury, Wiltshire SP3 5QP

CHOOSE A PHOTOGRAPH
CHOOSE A PHOTOGRAPH
FROM THIS BOOK

Voucher *for* ***FREE*** *and Reduced Price Frith Prints*

Please do not photocopy this voucher. Only the original is valid, so please fill it in, cut it out and return it to us with your order.

Picture ref no	Page no	Qty	Mounted @ £7.49	Framed + £14.95	Total Cost £
		1	Free of charge*	£	£
			£7.49	£	£
			£7.49	£	£
			£7.49	£	£
			£7.49	£	£
			£7.49	£	£
			* Post & handling		£2.25
			Total Order Cost		£

Please allow 28 days for delivery.
Offer available to one UK address only

Title of this book ....
I enclose a cheque/postal order for £ ....
made payable to 'The Francis Frith Collection'

OR please debit my Mastercard / Visa / Maestro / Amex card, details below

Card Number

Issue No (Maestro only) Valid from (Maestro)

Expires Signature

Name Mr/Mrs/Ms ....
Address ....
....
....
.... Postcode ....
Daytime Tel No ....
Email ....

ISBN 1-85937-959-1 Valid to 31/12/07

Free Print - see overleaf

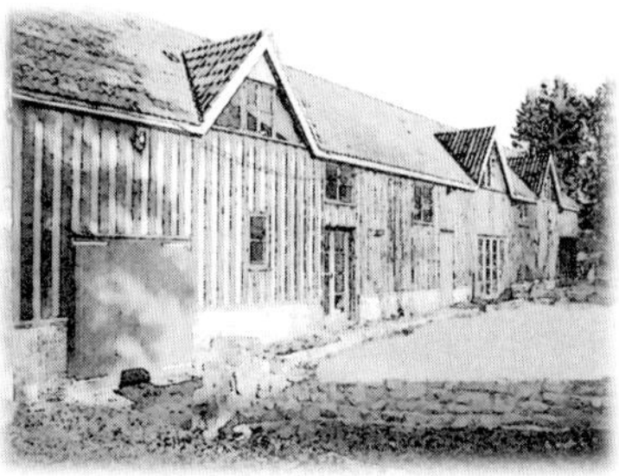

Would you like to find out more about Francis Frith?

We have recently recruited some entertaining speakers who are happy to visit local groups, clubs and societies to give an illustrated talk documenting Frith's travels and photographs. If you are a member of such a group and are interested in hosting a presentation, we would love to hear from you.

Our speakers bring with them a small selection of our local town and county books, together with sample prints. They are happy to take orders. A small proportion of the order value is donated to the group who have hosted the presentation. The talks are therefore an excellent way of fundraising for small groups and societies.

Can you help us with information about any of the Frith photographs in this book?

We are gradually compiling an historical record for each of the photographs in the Frith archive. It is always fascinating to find out the names of the people shown in the pictures, as well as insights into the shops, buildings and other features depicted.

If you recognize anyone in the photographs in this book, or if you have information not already included in the author's caption, do let us know. We would love to hear from you, and will try to publish it in future books or articles.

Our production team

Frith books are produced by a small dedicated team at offices in the converted Grade II listed 18th-century barn at Teffont near Salisbury, illustrated above. Most have worked with the Frith Collection for many years. All have in common one quality: they have a passion for the Frith Collection. The team is constantly expanding, but currently includes:

Paul Baron, Phillip Brennan, Jason Buck, John Buck, Ruth Butler, Heather Crisp, David Davies, Louis du Mont, Isobel Hall, Lucy Hart, Julian Hight, Peter Horne, James Kinnear, Karen Kinnear, Tina Leary, Stuart Login, David Marsh, Lesley-Ann Millard, Sue Molloy, Glenda Morgan, Wayne Morgan, Sarah Roberts, Kate Rotondetto, Dean Scource, Eliza Sackett, Terence Sackett, Sandra Sampson, Adrian Sanders, Sandra Sanger, Julia Skinner, David Smith, Miles Smith, Lewis Taylor, Shelley Tolcher, Lorraine Tuck, Amanita Wainwright and Ricky Williams.